WADSWORTH PHI

ON

MERLEAU-PONTY

Daniel Thomas Primozic
Elmhurst College

WADSWORTH
—————*—————™
THOMSON LEARNING

Australia • Canada • Mexico • Singapore • Spain
United Kingdom • United States

WADSWORTH

THOMSON LEARNING

For Virginia, Helen, Claire, Thomas and Jeremiah

Printed in the United States of America
1 2 3 4 5 6 7 04 03 02 01 00

For permission to use material from this text, contact us:
Web: http://www.thomsonrights.com
Fax: 1-800-730-2215
Phone: 1-800-730-2214

For more information, contact:
Wadsworth/Thomson Learning, Inc.
10 Davis Drive
Belmont, CA 94002-3098
USA
http://www.wadsworth.com

ISBN: 0-534-57629-X

Contents

Contents

Preface

By any stretch of the imagination the philosophy of the existential phenomenologist, Merleau-Ponty has had and will have a deep and lasting impact upon our philosophical scene. He offers insightful and provocative descriptions of what it means to live as a person in the world. He asked essential and crucial questions about human life, scouted some fine new paths toward answers and reopens the gates of philosophy for us to enter. He has done us many other, more technical, philosophical favors as well. It is a delight to present a brief book about his work according to the sketch that follows.

I present the major moments of Merleau-Ponty's philosophy in a thematic manner. Given the nature of his philosophy, I think that he would prefer this mode of presentation. These themes are shown in the contexts of their historical development so that one can follow the maturation process for his key ideas. These themes revolve around a central core that is his theory of meaning: a theory of meaning that I see driving the entirety of his work and also a theory of meaning that provides a way to understand his work as a coherent whole. Hence, his theory of meaning is highlighted throughout this book.

In order to get the richest and most comprehensive picture of Merleau-Ponty's work, we also must understand the intellectual climate and contexts from which it emerged. Toward that end, I supply brief, introductory summaries concerning the relevant ideas of Descartes, Husserl, and Sartre with which Merleau-Ponty had struggled.

My hearty gratitude goes to Dr. Joseph Sathiaraj (Madras Christian College), Dr. Bill Hirstein (Elmhurst College), Mr. Joel Thompson (Elmhurst College) and Mrs. Virginia K. Primozic (beloved wife) for proofreading and editing help. Thanks go to my children and to my coworkers at Elmhurst College for their patience. Special thanks go to Dr. Daniel Kolak for his fine editorial guidance and his support of this project.

1

1
Early Work

Formative Years

Maurice Merleau-Ponty was born in1908 in Rochefort-sur-mer, France. He studied at the Ecole Normale Supérieure in Paris and took his *agrégation* in philosophy in 1931. While a student he was attracted to the ideas of the famous German phenomenologists of that time. Merleau-Ponty especially liked the work of Edmund Husserl after having heard his 1929 lectures in Paris, which later became Husserl's *Cartesian Meditations*. Merleau-Ponty also studied Heidegger and the later Husserl at the Husserl Archives at the Louvain in Belgium.

His first article, "Christianity and Ressentiment," appeared in *La Vie Intellectuelle* in 1935. There he reviewed Max Scheler's book, *Ressentiment*. He published another article for the same publication in 1936, called "*Etre et avoir*" (Being and Having), in which he reviewed Gariel Marcel's book of the same name. His next article (1936), called "*L' Imagination,*" appeared in the *Journal de Psychologie Normale*, and contained his review of Jean-Paul Sartre's book of the same name.

He wrote his first book, *The Structure of Behavior*, before serving as an officer in the French Army in the 1939-40 period of World War II. During the German occupation of France, Merleau-Ponty taught at Lycee Carnot in Paris and wrote his famous *Phenomenology of Perception*, published in 1945.

Also in 1945, Merleau-Ponty received appointments as Professor at the University of Lyon and then as Professor of Psychology at the Sorbonne in 1950. After the war, Merleau-Ponty co-founded and co-edited the publication, *Les Temps modernes*, with Jean-Paul Sartre and Simone de Beauvoir. In 1952 he accepted the prestigious Chair of Philosophy at the College de France and held that position until his death in 1961, leaving *The Visible and the Invisible* unfinished.

While still developing, Merleau-Ponty's thought was influenced by both philosophy and psychology. His philosophical life began by flying in the face of Descartes' dualism and his psychological research was born as a cut against the behavioral psychology of his time.

Descartes' Dualism

In his *Meditations on First Philosophy*, Rene Descartes created a metaphysical and an epistemological problem (a problem concerning our views of reality, knowledge and truth) from which we have scarcely recovered. There within the pages of that seventeenth century philosophical benchmark that gave rise to Modern Philosophy, Descartes wrote what has been called a *thought experiment* on his way toward establishing the kind of certainty necessary to establish firm and permanent structure in the sciences.

In his thought experiment, Descartes seeks absolute, indubitable certainty through a method of profound and exceptional doubt. Briefly put, Descartes thought the surest and the most cautious route to gaining knowledge was to doubt everything until one confronts an absolutely indubitable experience or entity, where doubt is no longer necessary nor fruitful.

While using this method of doubt, Descartes finds that he can doubt many things about his body and the empirical realm, available to the senses. Descartes says:

> All that up to the present time I have accepted as most true and
> certain I have learned either from the senses or through the
> senses; but it is sometimes proved to me that these senses are
> deceptive, and it is wiser not to trust entirely to any thing by
> which we have once been deceived. [1]

Descartes recalled times when he believed he was upright in his chair, writing upon his table before his study fire. He asks us, however, to recall also those astounding moments when our obvious sensate experiences are found to be merely false assumptions on our part.

> How often has it happened to me that in the night I dreamt that
> I found myself in this particular place, that I was dressed and
> seated near the fire, whilst in reality I was lying undressed in
> bed! At this moment it does indeed seem to me that it is with
> eyes awake that I am looking at this paper; that this head
> which I move is not asleep, that it is deliberately and of set
> purpose that I extend my hand and perceive it; what happens
> in sleep does not appear so clear and distinct as does all this.

But in thinking it over this I remind myself that on many occasions I have in sleep been deceived by similar illusions, and in dwelling carefully on this reflection I see so manifestly that there are no certain indications by which we may clearly distinguish wakefulness from sleep that I am lost in astonishment. And my astonishment is such that it is almost capable of persuading me that I now dream. [2]

So Descartes doubted all that came from his senses and his body. And, worse yet, to be sure that he arrived at absolute certainty, he raised this doubt to the level of an all powerful, cosmic *evil genius* whose business it was to always deceive Descartes and the rest of humanity and prevent any certainty whatsoever.

Therefore, to be careful and rigorous, Descartes assumed that he was always being deceived by his senses. By so doing, however, Descartes severely undermined the body's sense data and its ability to give us certainty and truth. And, in turn, Descartes eliminated the common sense, empirical approach to knowing truths concerning reality because of its unreliable nature. Descartes severs our very need for a body in the pursuit of truth when he says:

I suppose, then, that all the things that I see are false; I persuade myself that nothing has ever existed of all that my fallacious memory represents to me. I consider that I possess no senses; I imagine that body, figure, extension, movement and place are but but the fictions of my mind. What, then, can be esteemed as true? . . . I myself, am I not at least something? But I have already denied that I had senses and body. Yet I hesitate, for what follows from that? Am I so dependent on body and senses that I cannot exist without these? But I was persuaded that there was nothing in all the world, that there was no heaven, no earth, that there were no minds, nor any bodies: was I not then likewise persuaded that I did not exist?[3]

Descartes' thought experiment leaves him in a philosophical position that forces him to doubt everything because he may always be deceived by his senses and body. Descartes, thus, feels compelled by reason to rely the bodiless mind (rationalism) as his chance for gaining even one piece of certain knowledge and truth: his foundation for the sciences.

of a surety I myself did exist since I persuaded myself of something [or merely because I thought of something]. But there is some deceiver or other, very powerful and very cunning, who ever employs his ingenuity in deceiving me.

Then without doubt I exist also if he deceives me, and let him deceive me as much as he will, he can never cause me to be nothing so long as I think that I am something. So that after having reflected well and carefully examined all things, we must come to the definite conclusion that this proposition: I am, I exist, is necessarily true each time that I pronounce it, or that I mentally conceive it. . . But what then am I? A thing which thinks [*Cogito* or "I think"]. [4]

By proclaiming that he really did not need the senses to gain truth, he separated the mind from the body in a way that made of them two separate and distinct substances, almost two distinct "selves" that were so very different that it became difficult to understand how a thinking, invisible substance like the mind could ever interact, especially harmoniously and effectively, with the visible substance of our body. This *dualism* became not only a problem for Descartes to resolve but, more importantly for the history of philosophy, it became a metaphysical and epistemological *mind-body problem* that has plagued philosophers for hundreds of years. For the rest of the history of western philosophy up to and including much of the twentieth century, the body would be suspect and the mind had to rescue us from its traps.

Merleau-Ponty's Resolution of Descartes' Dualism

Merleau-Ponty rejects Descartes' reliance exclusively on the rational mind to serve us truth. That rationalistic reliance reduces our experience of the world to a thin thought, idea or concept. It also fails to account for the thickness and ambiguities of the undeniable experiences that emerge from our sensing the interruptions between what we think and how the world is, and our thoughts and the thoughts of others. In short, Descartes' dualism and rationalism disqualified our bodies from the process of our knowing ourselves, each other, and the world.

Therefore, although throughout the whole of his adult intellectual life, Merleau-Ponty remained a faithful student of Descartes, he nevertheless saw good reason to reappropriate and correct Descartes' analysis radically. Merleau-Ponty chose to go beyond Descartes' *cogito* for a theory of mind that would more accurately, authentically and adequately account for the pre-reflective, non-conceptual, bodily features of our perceptions of the world and our transactions with one another. As Merleau-Ponty criticizes Descartes' version of the mental, inner *cogito*:

5

The *Cogito* was the coming to self-awareness of this inner core. But all meaning was *ipso facto* conceived as an act of thought, as the work of a pure *I*, and although rationalism easily refuted empiricism, it was itself unable to account for the variety of experience, for the element of senselessness in it, for the contingency of contents. Bodily experience forces us to acknowledge an imposition of meaning which is not the work of a universal constituting consciousness, a meaning which clings to certain contents. My body is that meaningful core which behaves like a general function, and which nevertheless exists, and is susceptible to disease. [5]

To complete this more adequate theory of mind, Merleau-Ponty pressed into service the phenomenology and the science of psychology of his time. Drawing upon psychology, Merleau-Ponty used *Gestalt* theory as a point of departure. Nevertheless, he thought that even *Gestalt* theory stopped short of an adequate application of the perception of wholes. From psychology also, Merleau-Ponty drew upon behaviorism's identification of the activities of the mind with brain states. His more detailed criticism of the shortcomings of behaviorism will be seen in the section on *The Structure of Behavior*.

The Structure of Behavior

Much of Merleau-Ponty's first work, *The Structure of Behavior* (1942) is devoted to a detailed critical discussion of physiological psychology and the attempt to provide on its basis a reductive explanation of behavior. In developing his argument, Merleau-Ponty draws on *Gestalt* psychology and especially K. Goldstein's *The Organism* that emphasizes the holistic features of the life of organisms. Merleau-Pony takes over Goldstein's holism and incorporates it into what he terms a 'dialectical' conception of the structures of behavior, according to which, as organisms evolve and become more sophisticated, higher forms of behavior develop which transform the life of the organism. So the new capacities characteristic of these higher forms are not simple additions to an otherwise unaltered neurophysiology. Instead, through a process of dialectical assimilation, these new capacities bring with them changes in the functioning of the underlying neurophysiology. [6]

In his *Structure of Behavior*, Merleau-Ponty studies the behavior of plants, animals and human beings. He tries to analyze these by employing the scientific (causal) explanation of behavior. However, he finds that way of analysis unsatisfactory because it does not allow us to

6

see the behaving organism (especially a human being) as a center and focal point of meaning and not just as a static and inert variable in a mechanistic causal process. When trying to understand the behavior of human beings, the strict stimulus-response model of behaviorism is not adequate to the task, mainly because we are usually free to act in ways that are surprising and indeterminate.

In this work, Merleau-Ponty begins to develop the idea of the human being as a *body subject* – as an irrevocable, dialectical composite of both body and mind. This is an idea that he cultivates slowly toward a mature version in his later work.

The Dialectic

For us to understand his more mature work, however, we must go further than his attack upon reductionistic physiological psychology (behaviorism) to Merleau-Ponty's aforementioned use of a dialectical approach to the dualisms latent in such oversimplified, scientific analyses.

Merleau-Ponty's more inclusive and accommodating dialectical approach allows him to avoid the traps of inadequate or incomplete analyses that are the legacy of the false "either/or" reductionisms. For Merleau-Ponty, human life cannot be satisfactorily examined from the set of presuppositions that include the dualism of mind and body and subject and object. These dualisms usually leave out the body and its key role in the acquisition of knowledge. He asserts that "man is not a rational animal. The appearance of reason and mind does not leave in tact a sphere of self-enclosed instincts in man." [7] There is no clear separation of mind and body as they exist. Bodily life is ridden with the mental, and the mental is encrusted in the bodily. For example, I move my fingers around this keypad because I have a specific idea in mind that I want to capture within this passage. I first gained that idea through complex bodily movements and activities. My idea is purposefully signaled to movements of my hands on the keypad that create meaningful and coherent symbols that, in turn, will hopefully transmit those meanings to the reader. Thus, a complete and rigorous understanding of human behavior must take this dialectical relationship of the mind and body into account and must proceed from its platform, since it is the most adequate description of the phenomenon of human behavior. He speaks in favor of his new approach to his theory of mind: "but the new notion [concerning behavior] could receive its philosophical status only if causal or mechanical thinking were abandoned for dialectical thinking."[8]

Merleau-Ponty was impressed by behaviorist theories concerning the identity of mental activities with the overall functioning of the human body. Yet, he parts ways with those theories given their emphases on strictly one-sided, causal and quantitative analyses and measurements. And, "he is equally dissatisfied with such philosophical solutions as the idealistic or 'critical' philosophy of Brunschvicg or its opponent, 'naturalism.' "[9]

Again, according to Merleau-Ponty, none of these reductionistic, albeit "scientific," theories is satisfactory for the task of studying behavior because none of them realizes that the living, behaving organism (especially of the human variety) is a center of the meanings of those causal and mechanical processes which befall it. In short, the theories Merleau-Ponty criticizes in this work simply ignore and neglect a very important realm for the human subject: that of meaning. So behavior must be examined through a more adequate, dialectical and phenomenological method. And to do that adequately, we must study the many meanings of the body:

> There always comes a moment when we withdraw from a
> passion, driven by lassitude, exhaustion or self-love. The
> duality is not a simple fact but has the character of a principle,
> for every integration presupposes the normal functioning of
> subordinate formations, which always tend to their own well-
> being. However, there is no question here of a duality of
> substances. In other words, the concepts 'soul' and 'body'
> must be rendered relative. There is, first, the body as a mass
> of chemical combinations which constantly interact; then, the
> body as the dialetics of the living being and its environment;
> also the body as the dialetics of the social subject with its
> group; even all out habits may pass as an untouchable body for
> the 'I' of every moment. Each of these grades is 'soul' with
> respect to the lower grades, and 'body' with respect to the
> higher grades. The body in general is a whole of already
> established paths, already acquired powers, it is the acquired
> dialectic soil on which higher formation takes shape, and the
> soul is the new meaning that comes into existence. [10]

Merleau-Ponty turns to Husserl's phenomenology for this more adequate and accommodating method. Although he eventually finds fault with that methodology, it is useful for us, first, to see what Merleau-Ponty learned in his study of Husserl.

A Teacher of Perception: Husserl's Contribution to the Philosophy of Merleau-Ponty

Merleau-Ponty's debt to Edmund Husserl's phenomenological method is profound. We provide a brief terminological sketch of Husserl's method so we can understand its impact on Merleau-Ponty might obtain. [11]

Phenomenological Method

Edmund Husserl established the *phenomenological movement* with some major ends in view. Husserl wanted his new method of knowing and of talking about human experience to be a *radical* way of thought. He wanted the phenomenological method to divide us from our all-too-familiar ways of perceiving, thinking and behaving. Thus, he geared his phenomenology to help us see the world anew – from a rashly different set of perspectives – so that the presuppositions we ordinarily take for granted (*natural attitude*) can be realized, examined and perhaps be overcome if necessary. For Husserl, phenomenology was a tool for living the examined life and for gaining a clear, presuppositionless viewpoint.

Husserl also wanted his method to be rigorously scientific and comprehensive in scope. He wanted us to be aware of the important role our presuppositions play in our ways of approaching our interactions with the world and our ways of describing our lived-experiences (*Erlebnisse*) in the life-world (*Lebenswelt*).[12] He believed that an inquiry is legitimate or genuinely scientific only to the extent that it searches into its own set of presuppositions (those hidden, fundamental beliefs that guide and shape all that we are and do in our lives). An inquiry, according to Husserl, is rigorous to the extent that every move in the process of this inquiry is noted and accounted for, so that an intersubjective scrutiny of the procedure can obtain and an intersubjective judgment can be made as to the validity and value of the inquiry. He proposes his phenomenological method for accomplishing those goals. Merleau-Ponty aptly describes the essence of this method in his famous "preface" to *Phenomenology of Perception*:

> What is phenomenology? It may seem strange that this question has still to be asked half a century after the first works of Husserl. The fact remains that it has by no means

9

been answered. Phenomenology is the study of essences; and according to it, all the problems amount to finding definitions of essences; the essence of perception, or the essence of consciousness, for example. But phenomenology is also a philosophy which puts essences back into existence, and does not expect to arrive at an understanding of man and the world from any starting point other than that of their 'facticity'. It is a transcendental philosophy which place in abeyance the assertions arising out of the natural attitude, the better to understand them; but it is also a philosophy for which the world is always 'already there' before reflection begins – as an inalienable presence; and all its efforts are concentrated upon re-achieving a direct and primitive contact with the world, and endowing that contact with a philosophical status. It is the search for a philosophy which shall be a 'rigorous science', but it also offers an account of space, time and the world as we 'live' them. It tries to give a direct description of our experience as it is, without taking account of its psychological origin and the causal explanations which the scientist, the historian or the sociologist may be able to provide. [13]

Phenomenology aims to account comprehensively for the total *horizon* (or limits) of our lived-experience, of the only world that is before us, by trying faithfully and authentically to describe the *phenomena* (things as they are presented to human consciousness) that are constituents of that experience. It is designed, ultimately, to return us to "the things themselves," as they are experienced in the real, everyday world of finite human beings. It is designed to avoid the wishful and sometimes extravagant whimsy and presumptuous nature of the claims of many of the ancient, medieval and idealist philosophers of the past – presumptions and whimsies put to rest before, especially by the sword of skepticism wielded mightily by David Hume. In this sense, Husserl's method aimed at *realism*.

Radical Empiricism

In order to achieve these and other goals, Husserl developed the phenomenological method, which simply means "the study of phenomena." But are all of the various and multitude phenomena worthy of legitimate and rigorous study? This is why Husserl's phenomenology is often times compared favorably with the radical empiricism of William James. Their attitudes are the same toward what is worthy of examination in the human scope of experience. For both Husserl and James knowing and understanding are not passive perceptions but active manipulations of what is before us in perception and experience. Knowing and understanding are not mystical relationships with our world, but rather are a record of our interactions with our world. And, for both philosophers, that record must include all our interactions to be considered the complete and adequate record we like to call science.

The empiricist tradition, stemming from seventeenth century British philosophy, rejected the rationalism of influential philosophers like Descartes and the certainties and verities that he allegedly established exclusively through the use of his mind. The empiricists Locke, Berkeley and Hume pounded away at the largely unwarranted assertions of rationalism that were supposed to have firm and lasting foundations until they became what they always were: dogmas without sufficient evidence to support a scientifically healthy belief in them.

So these empiricists rallied around the notion that the source and legitimate basis of all claims to knowledge is experience itself: i.e., sensate experience. All our warranted theses and theories in science had to emerge from the domain of sense experience for them to have credibility and value.

But what is the basis, then, for our knowing the relations that connected our experiences. Would not those connections between our experiences have also to be experienced empirically to have scientific meaning and value? For example, if we insist, *contra* Hume, that we believe that we are selves that have an on going identity through time, would we not have to show empirically that my experiences as a child have direct connection and relationship to my experiences as a young and a middle aged man? Under the empiricist theory we would have to show exactly that for my belief in my own identity to have scientific weight and value. But, as Hume pointed out so forcefully, it is not possible to give empirical evidence for those relationships and, hence, Hume relegates such beliefs to the work of the smooth and easy passage of the mind and to the realm of the unscientific. Nevertheless, which of us realistically doubts that our memories of our past youth are ours and, therefore, we are really experience a direct connection to our pasts? But how do we account for those beliefs in a scientifically and empirically respectable way?

William James concludes that, indeed, we do experience these connections and relationships but, obviously, not with our senses. We must radically expand our notion of valid human experience beyond that of mere sense impressions and the ideas built upon them. As James says:

To be radical, an empiricism must neither admit into its constructions any element that is not directly experienced, nor exclude from them any element that is directly experienced. For such a philosophy, *the relations that connect experiences must themselves be experienced relations, and any kind of relation experienced must be counted as 'real' as anything else in the system. . . Radical empiricism,* as I understand it, *does full justice to conjunctive relations,* without, however, treating them as rationalism always tends to treat them, as being true in some supernal way, as if the unity of things and their variety belonged to different orders of truth and vitality altogether. [14]

For Husserl also anything whatsoever that becomes present to human consciousness qualifies as a legitimate "object" or "theme" of phenomenological analysis (description). To deny legitimacy to certain phenomena, as did the positivist philosophers of the twentieth century, is to expose a metaphysical presupposition that those phenomena are not "real enough" to be a meaningful slice of our life-world. But this is a contradictory notion, since it is clear that those very phenomena are ingredients in our life-world: to deny their importance is not to assure their non-existence.

Since it is an essential goal of this method to study the entire horizon of the life-world and these "orphaned" phenomena are, nevertheless, part of that horizon, they must be examined. For example, positivists might think that William James' study of *The Varieties of Religious Experience* a silly, meaningless domain of intellectual effort, and one unworthy of true science. Obviously Husserl would and James did disagree with that assessment for reasons already provided above. We simply cannot neglect any phenomena and still claim to give a comprehensive, rigorous, scientific picture of our experience.

According to Husserl's program for the phenomenological method, one of the chief ingredients is what he calls *epoche´*, "bracketing " or "the suspension of judgment." We gladly take for granted that our untutored, "natural" ways are adequate to the task of knowing our world. However, in order to really know whether they are adequate, we must somehow take leave of this natural attitude and scrutinize it "at arm's length," so to speak. We must stop taking for granted that our common sense, everyday perceptions of the world are good enough for us to call them rigorously scientific. For us to gain as much certainty as can be had, Husserl would have us perform *epoche´* and suspend (or hold in abeyance) our uncritical judgments concerning the phenomena we experience until we carefully and rigorously examine their natures and features from a more phenomenological, standpoint unclouded by presuppositions. This suspension is a stepping back from what we take for granted to a position where we look at our experience again from an attitude more attuned to that of a scientific researcher, who examines an object without prior expectations of what will be found. Within that general framework of "bracketing" or *epoche'*, there are several levels or species of stepping back from the natural attitude. These levels begin with the "eidetic reduction."

Eidetic Reduction: Epoche'

At the level of the "eidetic reduction," Husserl seeks the thing itself, which for him are the "meaning-structures" of the given phenomenon. This mental focus called the "first reduction" allows us to pass from the world of facts to the realm of essences – from facts to ideas (or meanings). Husserl does not intend by "essence" anything like an empirical object. Rather, by "essence" Husserl means "pure generalities" which are empirical only in the sense of the *radical empiricism* of James – in the sense that all human experience is worthy of scientific scrutiny insofar as all human experience is somehow meaningful.

The *eidetic reduction* proceeds in the following fashion: one begins with a given, individual phenomenon as, for example, a house (whether actually perceived or wholly imagined). Aided by memory, perspectival variation and fanciful variation (literally turning the house around in one's imagination so that the various perspectives of the house can be seen), one changes characteristics (or features) of the phenomenon without making it cease to be what it is – without *essentially* changing it. For instance, one can change the color and shape of the windows of the house without it ceasing to be a house. One can change the size and texture of the walls of the house without making it cease to be a house. However, one cannot change the features of the house so radically as to make it a sewing machine and still have the object remain a house.

Husserl assures us that eventually the changeless, necessary, essential characteristics of the phenomenon manifest themselves. One seizes upon the essential character of the phenomenon by a creative, intuitive grasp. For Husserl, at this stage, we now know what the phenomenon is – not as it exists independently of us, but rather, as it is given to our consciousness.

Phenomenological Reduction

The next level, or reduction, is called the "phenomenological reduction." Here Husserl performs the phenomenological reduction "proper" by "bracketing Being," or, more simply, by suspending his concern for the ontological (reality) status of the phenomenon at hand. He insists upon this reduction in order to avoid *a priori* (prior to experience) decisions about such ontological status. Obviously, unchecked *a priori* judgments concerning the ontological status of the phenomenon would embroil him in equally unwanted presuppositions. Husserl believes that for us to accomplish a genuine and rigorous account for the *Lebenswelt* (the world of lived-experience), we must be sure never to neglect or ignore any of its constituents. Therefore, according to Husserl, the only way to gain this assurance is to suspend ontological judgments and proceed with a careful eidetic variation instead.

Though there are other reductions mentioned by Husserl as his work matured, those already described suffice to set the stage for the ways in which Merleau-Ponty made use of them. Closing this section on Husserl's impact on Merleau-Ponty, I will mention only one other crucial concept: the idea of *intentionality*.

Intentionality

When trying to explain the nature of the phenomenological reduction, Husserl begins by telling us about *intentionality*. Husserl's teacher, Franz Brentano, contributed this term to modern psychology after studying Aristotle's theory of intentionality: i.e., that all conscious acts are *directed* toward some object. In his *Psychology From An Empirical Standpoint*, Brentano concludes that reference to an object (of any sort, even an emotional object like joy) is indispensable to our conscious lives. He says that there is "No hearing without something heard, no believing without something believed, no hoping without something hoped, no striving without something striven for, no joy without something we feel joyous about, etc." [15]

Accordingly, Husserl maintains that consciousness is always consciousness *of something* and is, therefore, never void of content. That content, however, is not only grasped or collected from the object as it exists independently of our perceiving it. There are two poles in the structure of the process of knowing: the knower (epistemic subject) and the known (epistemic object). Thus, the content of consciousness is influenced also by perceptual viewpoint, presuppositions and by the perceptual peculiarities of our individual sense organs. This means that the character of the phenomenon is always co-determined by its mode of apprehension, or by the character of the individual conscious act through which the phenomenon presents itself. For example, our visual impression of a cup is influenced by our own, unique organs of sight and their peculiarities. So, a colorblind person will see, perhaps, a blue cup as gray. Hence, for Husserl, the essences of phenomena are both *grasped* and *created*.

If that is the case, the claims of "objectivity" advanced by empirical, positivistic science and the "objectivity" presupposed by the natural attitude are unwarranted and, therefore, cannot be held consistently let alone be taken for granted. Thus, the need for *epoche'* and phenomenological reduction becomes evident, especially in the work of Merleau-Ponty.

The Phenomenology of Perception: An Early Theory of Meaning

As was mentioned before, the early, dialectically driven themes presented in his *Structure of Behavior* find more maturity when later applied alongside a full blown phenomenological analysis of human experience as a body-subject. Merleau-Ponty offers that analysis in his major work of his early period: *Phenomenology of Perception* (1945, French edition; 1962, English edition). There he develops the notion of the *body-subject* in terms of the essential role the body plays in perception, knowledge and meaning.

For Merleau-Ponty, perception is not simply a conscious or cognitive event upon which we can train our reflective faculties. In many primordial and fundamental respects, perception is pre-conscious and pre-thematic (meaning those impressions that are concretely grasped by us before our minds take up this perception as an intellectual theme for consideration). In perception the body plays the predominant role.

The Intentional Arc

The first sections of the *Phenomenology of Perception* refute the idea that the perception of phenomena progresses according to an atomic model – a model that can be traced back to David Hume. That model of perception maintains that our concrete perceptual experience is built up from psychical elements that are united only through association and aided by memory and judgement. But, Merleau-Ponty realizes that phenomenal realities come to us as meaningful wholes or *Gestalten* – as phenomenal fields. These phenomenal fields contain both foregrounds and backgrounds of meaning and significance for us. As in any *Gestalt* phenomenon, these backgrounds and foregrounds trade predominance through our own willed shifts of focus. Hence, the meanings that attend those backgrounds and foregrounds shift along with the shifting perceptions.

Merleau-Ponty describes perception by using the idea of an "intentional arc," wherein both our intellectual and perceptive experiences presuppose the possibility of pointing our consciousness into wildly divergent directions. Merleau-Ponty explains this by using the metaphor of a projector or search light that can be turned and vectored in all directions, inside and outside.

In perception we have what he calls *motility*, or the capacity to train our "projectors" in all directions, inside and out, to situate ourselves in the world. Thus it is the body that is the pre-condition for all our experience – the pre-condition for the human epistemic subject, or more precisely, the *body-subject*, because the body makes motility possible.

> Beneath intelligence as beneath perception, we discover a more fundamental function, 'a vector mobile in all directions like a searchlight, one through which we can direct ourselves towards anything, in or outside ourselves, and display a form of behaviour in relation to that object.' Yet the analogy of the searchlight is inadequate, since it presupposes given objects on to which the beam plays, whereas the nuclear function to which we refer, before bringing objects to our sight or knowledge, makes them exist in a more intimate sense, for us. Let us therefore say rather, borrowing a term from other works, that the life of consciousness -- cognitive life, the life of desire or perceptual life -- is subtended by an 'intentional arc' which projects round about us our past, our future, our human setting, our physical, ideological and moral situation, or rather which results in our being situated in all these respects. It is this intentional arc which brings about the unity of the senses, of intelligence, of sensibility and motility. And it is this which 'goes limp' in illness. [16]

All our conscious life and the very *self* is made possible by this "intentional arc" that projects around us and situates us in our world: it presents our past, present, future, our human and non-human milieu, our physical situation, our ideological situation, our moral situation, etc. In short, it shows our bodies to be centers of all these vectors of meaning. We are *centers of meaning* and that is revealed especially by our body making it possible to change and vary our perceptual perspectives and, in turn, change and vary the attending meanings thereof.

Because of this "intentional arc" we can have an ongoing thread of meaning that stitches together the moments of our lives into an experienced unity of our persons, otherwise known as our personal identity. For instance, my living through all the seemingly disconnected moments of writing this book finds connection and unity, an intentional arc, through the meaning that I give to this pursuit so that the overall effort as lived by me seems a cumulative one – one called "this book."

The Body-Subject

Merleau-Ponty reckons that if that is the more adequate model of perception, then the body, or the *body-subject*, is the giver of the meanings that we carry through our lives. In short, we *are* our bodies and without them *we* would be impossible. Our consciousness, our experience and identities are found in and through our bodies. This, certainly is not what Descartes maintained, as has already been noted. The *body-subject* is revealed as that pre-condition and faculty of meaning-bestowing acts. Without the body-subject we would cease to be and so too would cease human experience, life, knowledge and meaning.

This is mainly because insofar as the world becomes meaningful for us, insofar as we become meaningfully situated among the things of the world, phenomenal structures are not merely realities that are independent of us but are bound to our existence as body-subjects – as givers of meaning. As the body is *motile*, as it moves through, situates and orients itself in the world, the body gives meaning to that world of our human experience.

In the second part of this book, Merleau-Ponty devotes his time to the analysis of the perceived world. Here he shows that so-called "sensation" is already a form of perception, and therefore, of the formulation of ideas. He points to the fact that the senses are already "smart." Our minds and the ideas therein are already informing our senses which are tuned to feeding us specific kinds of data which can

17

be mentally processed. That data, in circular fashion, helps to make the senses "smart" in perception. Thus there is no such thing as mere "sensation" nor mere "reflection" as talked about by the British empiricists and their contemporary philosophical heirs. The perceptual world is more complex and more synthetic. Mind and body are much more intertwined than those other thinkers envisioned.

The Pre-Reflective Cogito: A Dialectical Approach

The middle and later sections of the book are devoted to showing that our conscious existence (what Descartes referred to as the "I think," the *cogito,* or what Descartes thought we really are: things that think) is rooted in a pre-conscious, pre-reflective *motility* – the body-subject. The most important sections are on his notion of the *pre-reflective cogito,* language and his theory of meaning.

Here Merleau-Ponty points out that what are held to be our purely cognitive meanings for words, terms or signs must come to us through a physical, bodily sensed mark or symbol: meaning that again the body plays a primordial role in the determination of human meanings. Symbols contain silent meanings that are perceived or are "spoken" through bodily processes and organs and become understood and meaningful for the "hearer."

Once the meaning of the symbol is grasped or "marked" by the hearer, the spoken meaning returns to the silence from which it came. However, there is something new that is added to the history or "career" of the symbol: i.e., the new meaning that the hearer has added to the word because of her new spatial, bodily, orientation toward the world – the new meanings that an individual brings to the word and the world. Hence, the meaning of terms also are dialectically, spatially and situationally driven as is everything else for Merleau-Ponty. The synthesis of new and pre-existing meanings for the symbols are then carried along within the on-going career of the linguistic symbol, thus giving it a kind of life or being of its own.

This dialectical, phenomenological method that allows us to take into view the whole of the behaving body-subject, including the meanings that events may have for that body-subject, comes especially from Merleau-Ponty's re-appropriation of Husserl's theory of meaning. Merleau-Ponty found Husserl's theory of meaning useful as a point of departure to gain this forgotten soil of meaning. However, Merleau-Ponty also sees Husserl's analyses of meaning as somewhat wanting as well. Hence, in the *Phenomenology of Perception*, especially in his chapter on "The Cogito," Merleau-Ponty moves away from a strictly

18

Husserlian approach to a theory of meaning in order to reconstitute his own.

Husserl's Theory of Meaning

Edmund Husserl, in his *Logical Investigations*,[17] marks us as the creators of the meaningfulness of signs. He maintained that we *constitute* the meanings of signs. We do that by meaning-conveying-acts which find their completion and corroboration in meaning-fulfilling-acts. Signs (marks, words, symbols) themselves have no meaning until we bestow our intention upon them.

Even so, in Husserl's theory of meaning, the physical mark or sign has no necessary connection to the meaning we have given it. I still am free to choose one of many possible words upon which I can confer my meaning. However, according to Husserl, I am not free to alter the "essential structure" of the meaning I would convey. That essential structure should remain as stable, immortal and unchanging as a Platonic *eidos* (form, essence, or the defining principle at work in a thing that makes that thing what it is). He believed that there is an essential meaning in language that does not change or vary – an *eidetic* or essential character for expression that is universal, eternal and immortal. Only the modes of the expression in differing languages, for instance, are subject to change. For Husserl, "A linguistic expression is not the passing of a physical phenomenon [or a mark, a sign] but an ideal structure that is capable of "being again." [18]

It is possible to know, for example, that both the English term, "table," and the German term, "*Tisch*," have the same meaning though their modes of linguistic expression (or signs) are clearly different. Here Husserl seems quite Platonic indeed, because for both Plato and Husserl the meaning of both signs remains constant and unchanging despite the dissimilarity of their linguistic expressions. Husserl felt that it is, precisely, this ideal structure of language that allows any linguistic communication whatsoever.

Again, it must be recalled that for Husserl, *we* confer meanings upon signs or words. We constitute the word's meaning by a "meaning-conveying act" (an intentional act by which we bestow meaning upon a term). Later, we try to complete it with a "meaning-fulfilling act" (an intersubjective, corroborative act wherein we as a group of language users agree that a term will have a specific meaning). In short, we are the creators of meaning and the linguistic sign itself has no meaning until we intend one for it. The physical word or sign itself has no necessary or important connection with the meaning that I bestow upon it. I am free to choose any one of many possible words upon which I may bestow a specific meaning.

However, I am not free to change the essential structure of the meaning I try to convey with this rather arbitrary choice of linguistic marks. That "meaning-structure" must remain stable and unchanged or else it is not the *real* structure I am attempting to communicate. In Husserl's view, the thought behind the sign is distinct from the sign itself.

Additionally, the thought or meaning behind the sign is viewed as lying in our interior of consciousness and the sign is seen as an external, physical phenomenon. Since, for Husserl, the thought is considered to be prior to the word and, thus, does not *need* the word: the thought has an absolute, eternal, *eidetic* and autonomous nature. This can be seen clearly in Husserl's discussion of interior monologue:

> Or shall we say that, even in solitary mental life, one still uses expressions to intimate something, though not to a second person? Shall one say that in soliloquy one speaks to oneself, and employs words as signs, i.e., as indications, of one's own inner experiences? I cannot think such a view acceptable. Words function as signs here as they do everywhere else: everywhere they can be said to point to something. But if we reflect on the relation of expression to meaning, and to this end break up our complex, intimately unified experience of the sense-filled expression, into the two factors of word and sense, the word comes before us as intrinsically indifferent, whereas the sense seems the thing aimed at by the verbal sign and meant by its means. [19]

Merleau-Ponty's Early Theory of Meaning

After lengthy study and reflection, Merleau-Ponty finds Husserl's analysis of meaning lacking. Through examinations of his own lived experience, Merleau-Ponty discovered that there was a sense in which the meaning of a word and its symbolic manifestation share a unified existence, like the mind and body, especially in the process of perception. The being of the sign and the being of the meaning are one being. Even so, for Merleau-Ponty the meaning structure invested in the sign is carried with the sign, yet can be changed and varied over time – allowing for the evident "growth" of the meanings of words.

In his chapter of *Phenomenology of Perception* [20] called "The Cogito," Merleau-Ponty provides reason to think Husserl's position on meaning untenable. He appeals to our "primitive consciousness" for which a word or sign not only suggests a situation in its audience, but also *evokes* that situation for that audience of this expression. For example, for me the words "child birth" evoke the very situations, feelings and emotions of the births of my children. Those words and signs powerfully bring me to vivid, concrete, lived meanings through which I mentally and emotionally live again the situations of the births of my children.

Merleau-Ponty realizes that the awareness of human existence itself has its origin in *ek-stase*, "the active transcendence of the subject in relation to the world,"[21] the self-transcending movement of the "body-spirit," or our primordial movement out toward the world. Merleau-Ponty claims that we can know of our own existence only because of a kind of "perceptual faith" (that there is something to be perceived) built upon a primordial experience of the existence of the world. This perceptual faith is a pre-condition for all meaning. He says that: "It is through my relation to 'things' that I know myself; inner perception follows afterwards." [22]

Again Merleau-Ponty sees a need to reinterpret even Husserl in order to avoid the intrinsic duality of fact and essence that Husserl promotes in his eidetic theory of meaning. If Merleau-Ponty can show that speech or language conveys perceptual experience and not merely abstract thought, it will help him to establish his claim that neither we, nor our meanings, are ethereal, eidetic "subjects" or structures. Rather, both we and our meanings are very well integrated wholes, or centers of meaning. And also he can establish that we, as conscious-bodies, are able to see and talk about our experiences of the things themselves given through our primordial contact with the world. Consequently he needs to show that there is an indivisible interconnection between thinking and speaking and between thought and our perception of things.

The Schneider Case

Merleau-Ponty draws upon the work of the *Gestalt* psychologist, K. Goldstein to show that the body-subject is the giver of our human meanings, and not an aloof, detached, constituting, Husserlian, Transcendental Ego. Merleau-Ponty achieves this by taking an example of a patient called Schneider from Goldstein's work. Schneider was a World War I veteran who sustained brain injuries from combat. His perception was limited to what he presently was doing. His attention could be drawn to nothing else – neither past nor future life events. He clearly had no unified cohesive threads of meaning in his life. He was a living, pathological version of the Humean paradigm of an atomic self with no on-going personal identity or internal connection. Merleau-Ponty discovered that Schneider's "intentional arc" broke down. He was incapable of being bored. Briefly, Schneider was incapable of having a life "project."

> So in Schneider's case disability is not merely neurophysiological; nor is it just a disorder of a consciousness detached from behaviour; instead it bears witness to the normal personal union of mind and body through which a form of intentionality is expressed in unreflective but organized bodily movement. Once the further step is taken of recognizing that this is the basic form of intentionality, it follows that the phenomenological perspective itself needs to be relocated from the personal sphere of explicit thought to the sub-personal domain of bodily movement . . . [23]

Schneider's case is intended to show that a malfunction of the body-subject (especially in Schneider's case, the brain) was the cause of Schneider having no ongoing self identity. It is the ultimate source of our situation. It orients us toward the world and arranges the world and contexts that spin around it. As Merleau-Ponty says:

> To sum up, what we have discovered through the study of motility, is a new meaning for the word 'meaning' . . . Bodily experience forces us to acknowledge an imposition of meaning which is not the work of a universal constituting consciousness, a meaning which clings to certain contents. My body is that meaningful core which behaves like a general function, and nevertheless exists, and is susceptible to disease. In it we learn to know that union of essence and existence which we shall find again in perception generally, and which we shall then have to describe more fully.[24]

Merleau-Ponty's use of the Schneider case demonstrates that the body-subject, and not a mere constituting consciousness, is the giver of human meaning. One is always the body-subject and is never an ethereal, free floating, transcendental ego. This was so even in the pathological case of Schneider.

The Reconstitution of Meaning: The Reconstituted Cogito

Merleau-Ponty claimed that meanings, words, and language predate our meaning-bestowing acts. They come before us pre-constituted, with a history and a kind of life of their own. I re-constitute these meanings when I read them, interpret them from my temporal and spatial presuppositions, and add my meanings and new life to the word and also to the concept.

Phenomenologically, the words and meanings pre-exist me. They have the power to evoke in me a new and hitherto unexperienced thought or viewpoint concerning the world. Merleau-Ponty puts it this way:

> The *cogito* [Descartes'] is either this thought which took shape three centuries ago in the mind of Descartes, or the meaning of the books he left for us, or else an eternal truth which emerges from them, but in any case is a *cultural being* of which it is true to say that my thought strains towards it rather than embraces it, as my body, in a familiar surrounding, finds its orientation and makes its way among objects without needing to have them expressly in mind. [25]

The word, *cogito*, has its own being and its own powers. It already had a meaning structure of "I think" when it was re-invested with Descartes' own, special meaning honed for his specific epistemological project. It already has a life of its own when I read it in Descartes work and it is something toward which I must *strain* to grasp. I strain so much, in fact, that I tend to lose myself in grasping Descartes' meaning for *cogito*: "my consciousness takes flight from itself and, in them [the meanings], is unaware of itself." [26]

It is important to realize the conflict this assertion has with Husserl's viewpoint. Were Merleau-Ponty correct on this point, then, that the word already has lived an on-going life of meaning of its own, then the word already comes to us with a history or "career" of its own. When we come to interpret the meaning of the word, we *invade* its being and leave something of a contribution of our own to its continued life of meaning. We grasp the meaning already there in the word and attach or create our own meanings for the word. In reading Descartes' *cogito*, we add to his meaning the meaning that was *evoked* in us. Thus, we do not constitute words, as Husserl would have us believe. For Merleau-Ponty, we *re-constitute* them.

Reconstitution occurs when we re-orient the meaning of a word by making it meaningful to and *for us* – by *speaking* it. We bring the being of the word into our situation and see it residing *here*, with us.

We bring it into our time and space. And so we help words grow and live, just as they help us to do likewise.

The sign itself bears with it a history of human interpretations and meaning-structures. In the case of some ancient words, they are the cumulative effect of generations of denotative and connotative reconstitution. Words are "becoming" because their meanings do not stay in quiet retirement but, instead, are "worked" and are changed with time. The meanings of words are as temporal as their significations are spatial.

The Becoming of Language

Implied in this is that language is yet another being, another center of meaning which exists in time and in space. As such, language is a phenomenon for which we must give some account – hopefully, from Merleau-Ponty's viewpoint, an account of the whole of the being of language. In any case, he has argued that we cannot view meaning as Husserl would have it: as static, essential, meaning-structures unconnected to the spatial and temporal flow of living beings. For Merleau-Ponty meanings move as beings move. They both live, grow, degenerate and both can die.

So, contrary to Husserl, Descartes' *cogito* is not one static, eidetic being. It, like all of us, is more of a *becoming*. To Merleau-Ponty the *cogito* is as many things as those who read it, think it, write it and understand it. It is a thought, a meaning, a truth, a Cartesian epistemological device, and also, most strikingly, a *cultural being* much like himself, much like the paper under his hand and the trees outside his window. *It is something* toward which he throws himself, something that pre-exists him, something that has a life of its own, something that he strains to perceive, and something in which he loses himself (in thinking about Descartes' philosophical agenda for writing the term, *cogito*) and also finds himself (in a realization of his own *cogito* which Descartes writing evokes).

Merleau-Ponty goes further to point out that the 'becoming of language" is not just a case of translating one cultural-historical way of reconstituting meaning into a different cultural-historical way of reconstituting the *same* meaning. *The meaning, too, changes.* The way we express our meanings affects the meanings themselves. We attach fresh, different meaning to the word. If our expressions are truly and intentionally expressions *of something,* the words must be seen as intentional *orientations.*

Therefore, the words cannot be (as Husserl wanted them) severed from the meanings that those words are chosen to convey. Speech, words, or authentic expression, as they are lived, express *something* and make that something present to us, both to the author and the audience. The way in which meanings are made present to us tends to depend upon the words we use to express our meanings. Certain cultural expressions are more successful for this than are others. This shows that there is an interdependence between that which we try to convey and the manner in which we try to convey it. Each affects the other.

A Child's Story

Merleau-Ponty provides an example of a story, told in a children's book, of the disappointment felt by a small boy who put on his grandmother's glasses and took up her book fully expecting, with that, he would be able to read and enjoy the stories she had read him. He was disappointed that the stories were not there to be had and because he only saw black marks on the white paper. For Merleau-Ponty's purposes, the moral of the story is that the child mistook the being and power of language only as being the ritual the grandmother enacted by her physical movements, gestures and reading tools. Nothing happened for the child because he thought that the meaning of the story was in the enactment of the ritual and was not aware that it was in the words being chosen, read and spoken. The child thought that the simple performance of mere rituals was enough to produce the magical world that is the story. By merely mimicking an empty, meaningless ritual, the child could not evoke a situation, an orientation.

Merleau-Ponty wants us to know that "evoking a situation" is no less magical for adults:

> The power possessed by language of bringing the thing
> expressed into existence, of opening up to thought new ways,
> new dimensions and new landscapes, is in the last analysis, as
> obscure for the adult as for the child. In every successful
> work, the significance carried into the reader's mind exceeds
> language and *thought as already constituted is* magically
> thrown into relief during the linguistic incantation, just as the
> story used to emerge from grandmother's book. [27]

Merleau-Ponty discovered that the evocative power of language itself allows us to "forget" both the visible words and their invisible, intended meanings and, in turn, allows us to invest the words new meanings from our lives, from our own time and being. In the case of

Descartes' *cogito*, we make of Descartes' cultural-historical "I think" our own cultural-historical "I think."

For example, Descartes lived in seventeenth century France and Holland, and likely wore a sword as he walked through city streets. He wrote his famous *cogito* with a quill and had it widely published on pages type-set by hand. He proclaimed his *I am* from that cultural-historical milieu.

Centuries later, and in another language, I read his *cogito* and when I understand it, I begin to lose it to my own *cogito,* my own *I am.* I read and understand it and begin to invest it with my own existence, my own situation: surrounded by computer equipment, books, and no swords. It was his *cogito* that evoked mine: as his becomes lesser mine becomes greater. That is the mediating feature of language.

The mediating feature of language gives us the illusion, however, of an eternity of meaning because we *seem* to experience Descartes' *cogito.* But, of course, we cannot. His words evoke in us our own *cogito,* at which point the word *cogito* has taken on a similar but not, in any way, an identical meaning. It is mine and not his. I am not Descartes, nor do I have the pleasure of his viewpoint of the world. I am not his body nor do I have his orientation. I am my orientation, body and viewpoint. My situation and his are quite different though they share some similarities. Therefore, my *cogito* is new, even though evoked by his.

To deny this, as Husserl does, is to remove the factical (or that which is irrevocably factual about us) from the world. For Husserl to deny it is to remove us from our bodily, situated, orientations. It is to remove us from our bodies to a disembodied, transcendental ego – a "for-itself," or an absolute, pure consciousness, without the bodily precondition for experience *per se.* To do that is to deny a fundamental fact of our existence: i.e., existence itself. Therefore, the "intellectual" understanding of which Merleau-Ponty accuses Husserl cannot yield any concrete knowledge of the magical, pre-reflective meaning of our relation to the world that is the fundamental fact of our existence – Husserl's understanding cannot yield information concerning the "pre-reflective," oriented, situated, concrete, lived *cogito.* Nor, therefore, does Husserl provide an adequate account of meaning itself.

Merleau-Ponty describes the moments of grasping and creating the meaning of Descartes' *cogito for us.* He maintains that we arrive at the *pre-reflective cogito* by first perceiving Descartes' sign for the *cogito* as a phenomenon in our world – and as a sign already bearing meaning along with it. As we begin to reconstitute its meaning, we open up what is being evoked in us: i.e., our own silent, primordial,

26

experience of the fact of ourselves. We experience a tacit, unspoken, *cogito* -- our pre-reflective, lived, experienced selves.

This primal experience of ourselves makes the *cogito* ours and makes it meaningful for us. We may then utter "I am, I exist" in a meaningful fashion: making the tacit, pre-reflective *cogito* a spoken, lived and, now, articulated concept that is coherent for us – making it a spoken, authentic *cogito*. It is lived through our speaking it, by our connecting our thought, body and speech through experience. As it turns out, then, the body and not pure consciousness, finds a new, complete, authentic meaning for the *cogito* by uttering the reappropriated term.

Our situated, bodily existence evokes an existence that presents itself to us and toward which we must strain out of ourselves through *ek-stase* (or a stretching away from oneself toward something else) – through our perceptual faith "that something is there." Thought and meaning come about through the existence of the sign, just as the awareness of ourselves comes about through our experience of the world – through *ek-stase*. It is our existence, then, our situation and our body-consciousness that yield meaning, Husserl's mere constituting (or creating a meaning) is not powerful enough to do so. As Merleau-Ponty puts this:

> If the subject *is* in a situation, even if he is no more than a possibility of situations, this is because he forces his ipseity into reality only actually being a body, and entering the world through that body. In so far as, when I reflect on the essence of subjectivity I find it bound up with that of the body and that of the world, this is because my existence as subjectivity is merely one with my existence as a body and with the existence of the world, and because the subject that I am, when taken concretely, is inseparable from this body and this world. The ontological world and body which we find at the core of the subject are not the world or body as idea, but on the one hand the world itself contracted into a comprehensive grasp, and on the other the body itself as a knowing body . . . We are in the world, which means that things take shape, an immense individual asserts itself, each existence is self-comprehensive and comprehensive of the rest. [28]

For the moment, we will pause in our look at Merleau-Ponty's reconstitution of Husserl. Husserl reappears especially in Merleau-Ponty's last work, *The Visible and the Invisible*.

[1] Rene Descartes, *The Philosophical Works of Descartes*, Volume I, translated by Elizabeth Haldane and G. R. T. Ross, Cambridge: Cambridge University Press, 1972, p. 145.

[2] *Ibid.*, pp. 145-146.

[3] *Ibid.*, p. 150.

[4] *Ibid.*, pp. 150-153.

[5] Maurice Merleau-Ponty, *Phenomenology of Perception*, New York: Humanities Press, 1962, p. 147.

[6] Thomas Baldwin, "Merleau-Ponty, Maurice, *Routledge Encyclopedia of Philosophy*, New York: Routledge, 1998, p. 321.

[7] Maurice Merleau-Ponty, *The Structure of Behavior*, Boston: Beacon Press, 1963, p. 181.

[8] *Ibid.*, p. 226.

[9] Herbert Spiegelberg, *The Phenomenological Movement: A Historical Introduction*, Second Edition, Volume II, The Hague: Martinus Nijhoff, 1976, p. 529.

[10] Remy C. Kwant's translation of pp. 226-227 of *La structure du comportement*, as seen in his *The Phenomenological Philosophy of Merleau-Ponty*, Pittsburgh: Duquesne University Press, 1963, pp. 46-47.

[11] For an excellent, crisp and more detailed description of Husserl's phenomenological method, see Victor Velarde-Mayol, *On Husserl*, United States: Wadsworth Publishing Company, 2000.

[12] The concept of the life-world or *Lebenswelt* necessarily a self evident one, so some explanation is needed. This term has a history that has been traced first to Schleiermacher's *Erlebnis* (lived experience) and then to Dilthey's *das Leben* (inner life). For a more complete understanding of this lineage see Howard N. Tuttle's *Wilhelm Dilthey's Philosophy of Historical Understanding: A Critical Analysis*, Leiden: E.J. Brill, 1969, pp. 12-20. These notions were later assimilated into the phenomenological concept of the *Lebenswelt*. Essentially, this term marks the general horizon or context of all human experience. It is the all-inclusive sphere of our finite, concrete experience that is presupposed by any human activity whatsoever. This pre-reflective (before reflective, intellectual analysis) world is given in our brute experience and serves as the material for our intellectual, metaphysical and epistemological articulations of that brute experience. This world is common to all of humanity and is pre-thematic (before a conscious and intellectual pursuit of an understanding of it) and pre-cultural (before cultural adaptations and interpretations of it). Hence, Husserl believed that this *Lebenswelt* could provide an objective and

universally valid basis for our scientific analyses and worldviews. Also
Husserl hoped that a phenomenological analysis of the contours of
Lebenswelt would avoid the perversions, reductionisms and sicknesses
which, for him, constitute the crisis in European science and humanity
in general.

[13] Maurice Merleau-Ponty, "Preface," *Phenomenology of Perception*,
New York: Humanities Press, 1962, p. vii.
[14] William James, *Essays in Radical Empiricism*, New York: E. P.
Dutton & Co., Inc., 1971, pp. 25-26.
[15] Franz Brentano, *Psychology From an Empirical Standpoint*, London
and New York: Routledge and Kegan Paul, 1973, p. 271.
[16] Merleau-Ponty, *Phenomenology of Perception*, pp. 135-136. The
"other works" quoted by Merleau-Ponty in this passage are
Hochheimer, *Analyse eines Seelenblinden von der Sprache, p. 49.*, and
Fischer, *Raum-Zeitstruktur und Denkstorung in der Schizophrenie*
respectively.
[17] Edmund Husserl, *Logical Investigations,* New York: Humanities
Press, 1970.
[18] Jitendranath Mohanty, *Edmund Husserl's Theory of Meaning*, The
Hague: Martinus Nijhoff, 1969, p. 31.
[19] Edmund Husserl, *Logical Investigations*, p. 279.
[20] Maurice Merleau-Ponty, *Phenomenology of Perception*, New York:
Humanities Press, 1962.
[21] Maurice Merleau-Ponty, *Phenomenology of Perception,* p. 70.
[22] *Ibid.* , p. 383.
[23] Baldwin, p. 322.
[24] Merleau-Ponty, *Phenomenology of Perception*, pp. 146-147.
[25] *Ibid.* , p. 369.
[26] *Ibid.* , p. 369. Brackets mine.
[27] *Ibid.* , p. 401.
[28] *Ibid.* , pp. 408-409.

2

The Middle Writings: Political Engagement

Merleau-Ponty and the "Engaged," True Philosopher

Merleau-Ponty's "middle period" is hall marked by intense socio-political engagement driven by the conditions in France in World War II. Thus, it is no wonder his intellectual products of that time concerned themes regarding the duty of the philosopher to find engagement in the world and community.

Merleau-Ponty's political engagement is seen clearly in the final sections of *Phenomenology of Perception*, where he analyzes the concept of freedom. From what has been said already, it should be no surprise that Merleau-Ponty found lived freedom in the *interworld*: a lived space between being and nothingness, self and world, and subject and object. Very simply, authentic human freedom is found in and through perception and the *body*.

The Body Politic

It is through an active, not inert, body that I am free to investigate and know my world. For instance, I now turn to the office window and now to the book I am reading, and then to children playing on the lawn. I know and will know more about my world through my body. The world knows and will know more about me through that same body that presents me.

We are, through our bodies, defining ourselves and are being defined by others. We perceive and are perceived through the publicity of our bodies. This way of existing is ambiguous, but it is our human way:

> There are two senses, and only two, of the word 'exist': one exists as a thing or else one exists as a consciousness. The experience of our own body, on the other hand, reveals to us an ambiguous mode of existing. . . . the body is not an object . . . . It is always something other than what it is always sexuality And at the same time freedom, rooted in nature at the very moment when it is transformed by cultural influences, never hermetically sealed and never left behind. Whether it is a question of another's body or my own, I have no means of knowing the human body other than that of living it, which means taking up on my own account the drama which is being played out in it and losing myself in it. I am my body, at least wholly to the extent that I possess experience, and yet at the same time my body is as it were a 'natural' subject, a provisional sketch of my total being. [1]

The self, then, is a synthesis (dialectical) of the world and the ego and it is lived through the human body. This body is public, and therefore, is also immediately social, material, and limited by its spatial and temporal conditions. Since that is so, our freedom is not absolute but rather is tempered and confined by our *situation*. Merleau-Ponty says:

> I am not an individual beyond class. I am situated in a social environment, and my freedom, though it may have the power to commit me elsewhere, has not the power to transform me instantaneously into what I decide to be. Thus to be a bourgeois or a worker is not only to be aware of being one or the other, it is to identify oneself as a worker or a bourgeois through an implicit or existential project which merges into our way of patterning the world and co-existing with other people. My decision draws together a spontaneous meaning in my life which it may confirm or repudiate, but not annul. [2]

Then what my body, my self, will mean to me will be the result of a communal project, of a political process. Merleau-Ponty develops his political philosophy within the spirit of dialectic, the truth of ambiguity, and a phenomenological analysis of the political structures of his era.

Merleau-Ponty's analysis of his political situation left him seeking mediation between the "humanism" (idealism, capitalism) and the "terror" (materialism and Stalinism) of his time. In his *Humanism and Terror* (French, 1947; English, 1969), he studies the problem of the communism of his milieu – a political system gone the way of absolute terror and oppression in the hands of Stalin. Merleau-Ponty contends that Marxist terrorism marks an essentially inhuman characteristic of Marxism itself, with its over-emphasis on materialism.

He looked for a third political position that would dialectically and synthetically mediate the false dilemma of bourgeois capitalism and Stalinistic communism. He also sought to leave room for mediation, interrogation and communication between these two, "cold war" conflicting, political moments. In that conflict, Merleau-Ponty advised peace and the intersubjective dialogue of real, concrete human beings – a dialogue built upon our primordial need for each other:

> Doubt and disagreement are facts, but so is the strange pretension that we all have of thinking the truth, our capacity for taking the other's position to judge ourselves, our need to have our opinions recognized by him to justify our choices before him – in short the experience of the other person as an *alter ego* in the very course of discussion. *The Human world is an open or unfinished system and the same radical contingency which threatens it with discord also rescues it from the inevitability of disorder and prevents us from despairing of it,* providing only that one remembers its various machineries are actually men and tries to maintain and expand man's relations to man. [3]

Merleau-Ponty's political writings came from the time in his life that he spent alongside Sartre and Simon de Beauvoir. But Merleau-Ponty and Sartre already worked as political allies and adversaries long before the war, dating back to their time as classmates at *Ecole normale* in the middle 1920's. Their friendship lasted until they broke over the politics of the Korean War of 1953.

Sartre remained communist despite the abhorrent actions of the North Korean communists. And because of those actions, Merleau-Ponty made a break with both communism and Sartre, calling him an *Ultra-Bolshevik.*

But the break with Sartre went deeper than their dispute about communism: it went to the conflict of how each man saw thew nature of philosophy itself and the methods thereof. So it is appropriate for us now to consider what Merleau-Ponty says about philosophy itself.

In Praise of Philosophy: The True Philosopher

> If the philosopher helps us to understand, henceforth,
> something of what a great man says in his own heart, he saves
> the truth for all, even for the man of action, who needs it, for
> no real statesman has seriously said that he was not interested
> in the truth. [4]

In Praise of Philosophy (1953) is a text taken from Merleau-Ponty's inaugural address delivered on the occasion of his acceptance of the Lavelle-Bergson chair of Philosophy at the *Collège de France*. In a prominent chapter of this short book, Socrates of Athens serves as the paradigmatic philosopher: one whose soul is fully engaged in the world and in his beloved community. Merleau-Ponty chooses Socrates to help him to provide definition and purpose for philosophy itself:

> The philosophy placed in books has ceased to challenge men.
> What is unusual and almost insupportable in it is hidden in the
> respectable life of the great philosophical systems. In order to
> understand the total function of a philosopher, we must
> remember that even the philosophical writers whom we read
> and who we are never ceased to recognize as their patron a
> man who never wrote, who never taught, at least in any
> official chair, who talked with anyone he met on the street,
> and who had certain difficulties with public opinion and with
> the public powers. We must remember Socrates.

That description of the engaged philosopher can serve also to characterize the way Merleau-Ponty saw his own duties of intellectual-political engagement during the war years and beyond. To that extent Merleau-Ponty patterned his political engagement after Socrates the philosopher, who also realized that absolute knowledge is impossible. That opens Socrates' mind to genuine truth – one that avoids dogmatic absolutism:

> The philosopher, it is said, should not prefer one rival
> dogmatism to another. He should occupy himself with
> absolute being beyond both the object of the physicist and the
> imagination of the theologian . . . Philosophy and absolute
> being are never above rival errors that oppose each other at
> any given time. These are never errors in quite the same way,
> and philosophy, which is integral truth, is charged with saying
> what in them it is able to integrate. In order that one day there

33

might be a state of the world in which free thought would be possible, of scientism as well of imagination, it did not suffice to bypass these two errors in silence . . . The philosophical absolute does not have any permanent seat. It is never elsewhere; it must be defended in each event. Alain said to his students: 'Truth is momentary for us men who have a short view. It belongs to a situation, to an instant; it is necessary to see it, to say it, to do it at this very moment, not before nor after in ridiculous maxims; not for many times, for there are no many times.' [5]

Merleau-Ponty saw that there were two forms of dogmatic absolutism in his time: dogmatic, uncritical, unthinking Christianity and dogmatic, unreflective, oppressive Marxism. He was intent upon trying to avoid both horns of dogmatism with Socrates' authentic kind of philosophy. He was dedicated to steering around those pitfalls despite the isolation one might feel from living outside the mainstream of one's social context – a context filled with mere dogmatic assertions.

This isolation, dialectically enough, binds the philosopher to living and feeling the ambiguities of life which are common to all people but are, nevertheless, profound. The philosopher sets herself apart in isolation from other people insofar as she realizes that life and its meanings are not clear cut, nor are they totally unclear. They are, instead, marked by a continuous reversal: a *Gestalt*-like process of unfolding and covering.

The philosopher is different from other people because she tries to articulate and share that mysterious, dialectical unfolding of layers of clarity and ambiguity. She tries to share publicly what should but cannot be shared: i.e., that utterly private and clear moment that, dialectically, becomes mysterious and ambiguous when shared. She tries to share what everyone already knows but declines to realize fully and to say:

> At the conclusion of a reflection which at first isolates him, the philosopher, in order to experience more fully the ties of truth which bind him to the world and history, finds neither the depth of himself nor absolute knowledge, but a renewed image of the world and of himself placed within it among others. His dialectic, or his ambiguity, is only a way of putting into words what every man knows well – the value of those moments when his life renews itself and continues on, when he gets hold of himself again, and understands himself by passing beyond, when his private world becomes the

common world. These mysteries are in each one of us as in him. What does he say of the relation between soul and the body, except what is known by all men who make their souls and bodies, their good and their evil, go together in one piece? . . . The philosopher is the man who wakes up and speaks. And man contains silently within himself the paradoxes of philosophy, because to be completely a man, it is necessary to be a little more and a little less than a man. [6]

Here the philosopher finds again the need for dialectic. He finds himself alone and yet cannot remain that way. Socrates could not simply retire and write scholarly pieces for narrow academic consumption. Socrates, the philosopher, knew that one could not merely be virtuous or happy in hiding:

> He was left with no other resource than himself . . . 'he drew away from the externally existent and retired into himself to seek there for the just and good' . . . But in the last analysis it was precisely this that he was self-prohibited from doing, since he thought that one cannot be just all alone and, indeed, that in being just all alone one ceases to be just. If it is truly the City that he is defending, it is not merely the City in him but the actual City existing around him. [7]

True, Socratic philosophy is a life of engaging the intellectual and the social milieu one inhabits. One must be in the world and act well within it for the common good and for the good of oneself. One must eliminate oppression and the dogmatism that spawns it. But one must do so philosophically and according to the obvious truths of our human condition of ambiguity. For Merleau-Ponty, there are no final answers and therefore no need for absolute, dogmatic philosophies or philosophers. The true philosopher is drawn by evidence and by complexity and ambiguity alike, by the search for absolute truth and by a suspicion of any that one may find. It is Socratic skepticism, or what Merleau-Ponty calls *interrogation*, that characterizes the true philosopher and has done so throughout history.

Sartre also maintained that line of thought. However, there also is a record of political struggle between Merleau-Ponty and Sartre that we will show briefly.

Merleau-Ponty and Sartre: Adventures of the Dialectic

Merleau-Ponty's *Adventures of the Dialectic* (French, 1955), was devoted to examining dialectical reason as it manifests itself in history. Along the way, Merleau-Ponty attacks what he sees as Sartre's destruction of the dialectic through the use of absolute and pure concepts – concepts not adaptable to the real use of dialectical reason. Here we see a break with Sartre that was in the making since Sartre's 1950 embrace of Bolshevism and that would deepen as time progressed.

Merleau-Ponty realized that the Marxism of his time, especially of the Communist Party, was a source of suspicion at best. The fact that Sartre joined the Communist Party only made Merleau-Ponty suspicious of Sartre as well. His disenchantment with communism and Sartre prompted the writing of *Les Aventures de la Dialectique* in 1955. Merleau-Ponty wrote that book because he wanted to finish with communism and show Sartre the error of his ways.

The grand philosophical difference between Merleau-Ponty and Sartre concerned the function and role *dialectic* played in the act of philosophy. In brief, because Sartre performed dialectical philosophy (coming from Hegel and Marx, essentially *both/and* reasoning and beyond dualistic *either/or* reasoning) poorly and incompletely, Merleau-Ponty considered Sartre's a *pseudo* dialectical analysis of our political lives: one that Merleau-Ponty called *truncated* and one that, therefore, yields false information about the political structures it was designed to study. This dispute foreshadows an ultimate parting of the ways for Sartre and Merleau-Ponty, one that we will see later.

In *Adventures of the Dialectic*, Merleau-Ponty demonstrates that Sartre had utterly failed to synthesize or unite his concept of radical freedom (our lives are our own free projects – a project of a *pure consciousness without being*) with Marx's materialist concept of history and society. Instead, Sartre tries to bind history onto his philosophy of absolute freedom of consciousness and freedom from the other – the other who alienates and who "is hell."

Merleau-Ponty sees that the reason that Sartre fails his own dialectical, materialist agenda comes down to Sartre's dualistic

36

ontology: a world composed of an *en soi,* or pure consciousness devoid of brute facts, and a *pour soi,* or pure being devoid of a free, constituting consciousness. For Merleau-Ponty, this Sartrean dualism was much too close to Descartes fatal mind-body dualism insofar as neither philosopher leaves room for mediation between the purity of their basic concepts. And insofar as there is no room for mediation, the dialectic is not possible because there is no possibility of its inevitable movement toward anything like Hegelian synthesis. For that possibility of dialectical movement, one's basic concepts must loosen and allow for the impurities of unification with their antitheses. They must allow for the *interworld*: this time of history.

Incarnate Political Consciousness

Merleau-Ponty's doctrine of incarnated consciousness establishes us as being in the world that has its own history: a world that we do not generate from ground zero, as Sartre would have us believe. Sartre got stuck in *either/or* thinking when he analyzed the concept of freedom. In any given situation, for Sartre, we either had total freedom or none at all, that freedom being the choice of what meanings we confer on our lived situations.

Merleau-Ponty knew that lived situations are more complex and ambiguous and demanding of dialectical thinking in order to accurately reflect them in our analyses. Each situation already comes to us with a whole history of meanings attached to it: meanings we cannot annul (facticity), like the fact that we live in *this flesh* in *this incarnation.* Hence, we are not totally free to choose all our meanings. The world presents us with situations already meaningful in ways that simply cannot be ignored.

For instance, I cannot ignore that I was born in a specific time slice and experienced what I could from the time and culture available to me in the second half of the twentieth century – a century already riddled and embedded with historical, political, economical, and spiritual meanings. I cannot change the *facticity* of my time and experience. Consequently, I am not free to choose any meaning whatever for my experience, but only those available to my time, culture and environment.

As far as Merleau-Ponty was concerned, Sartre was lodged snugly in the Cartesian version of the *cogito,* one that had no contact with the world of brute facts. Since Sartre's ontology implied that there could be no contact between the "I" and the world, the "I" could hardly be summoned into service for improving a human condition so terrifying in those days:

> During the occupation Merleau-Ponty learned how men are used by history. Each person has a social role; and, in an occupied country, anything he does, any public pronouncement he makes, is an action he performs as a citizen rather than an individual, affecting everyone – victor and vanquished alike. Not a person's intentions but the outcome of his acts are judged; no one's hands are clean. As soon as the war was over, Merleau-Ponty recorded these discoveries in the first issue of *Les Temps Modernes*: 'We were no longer permitted to be neutral in the combat. For the first time we were led not only to awareness but to acceptance of the life of society.' [8]

Sartre's philosophy can not help us to understand the true, concrete nature and actions of the proletariat or the relation of the workers to the Communist Party, because Sartre's philosophy prohibited an actual contact with that, or any, piece of the brute (and in that time, brutal) life-world.

In the end, Sartre took Merleau-Ponty's attacks on his philosophy so seriously that Sartre launched into a defense in the form of his own, vast, intricate, often brilliant and sometimes obscure analysis of the dialectic called *Critique of Dialectical Reason*:[9]

> Sartre accepted this criticism. As he remarks in his memorial article, 'It was Merleau who converted me . . . He taught me [about] that . . . action which since Hegel and Marx has been called praxis.' Sartre's *Critique of Dialectical Reason* shows he learned his lesson well. He echoes Merleau-Ponty in referring to his former existentialism as an 'ideology,' and he accepts (without acknowledgement) all of Merleau-Ponty's specific suggestions.[10]

So, Merleau-Ponty's long relationship with Sartre also was ambiguous. Both thinkers walked the same philosophical road for a while. Yet, they parted ways significantly on political issues both men considered crucial. They took each other seriously but found the other's philosophy both attractive and inspiring yet alien and quite mistaken. We will see Merleau-Ponty's final critique of and break with Jean-Paul Sartre later in this book.

[1] Maurice Merleau-Ponty, *Phenomenology of Perception*, p. 198.
[2] *Ibid.*, p. 447.
[3] Maurice Merleau-Ponty, *Humanism and Terror*, Boston: Beacon Press, 1969, p. 188.
[4] Maurice Merleau-Ponty, *In Praise of Philosophy*, Evanston: Northwestern University Press, 1963, p. 61.
[5] *Ibid.*, pp. 61-63.
[6] *Ibid.*, p. 63-64.
[7] *Ibid.*, p. 40.
[8] Hubert L. Dreyfus and Patricia Allen Dreyfus, "Translator's Introduction," of Merleau-Ponty's, *Sense and Non-Sense*, Evanston: Northwestern University Press, p. xxii.
[9] Jean-Paul Sartre, *Critique of Dialectical Reason*, London: NLB, 1976.
[10] Hubert L. Dreyfus and Patricia Allen Dreyfus, "Translator's Introduction," of Merleau-Ponty's, *Sense and Non-Sense*, p. xx.

3

The Last Work: The Visible and the Invisible

The Fulfillment of Husserl's Last Project

Maurice Merleau-Ponty began his philosophical itinerary in the shadow of Husserl and became one of the greatest phenomenologists. This itinerary was to lead him to a critical point when phenomenology and philosophy would become increasingly questionable to him. When Merleau-Ponty' life was abruptly interrupted in 1961, he was just in the process of finding a way to overcome the crisis of philosophy. [1]

In his famous, later work, *The Crisis of European Sciences and Transcendental Phenomenology*,[2] Husserl saw that a dangerous crisis of reason faced the socio-political world and also the science of his time. The status of reason was thrown into doubt. Subjectivism, relativism and nihilism were thought the better alternatives to it. Therefore, Husserl sought to save the use and status of reason and *episteme.*

Husserl performed his analysis of the *Crisis* in the three parts of that famous work. In the first part, Husserl defines the crisis of Western humanity and then sets forth an historical examination of the development of the *Crisis.*

Since, according to Husserl, the *Crisis* is based upon an unknowing betrayal of the ideal which constitutes Western civilization – the ideal, Cartesian-like vision of a universal knowledge grounded in reason (*mathesis universalis*) – that ideal must be retrieved for an adequate resolution of the *Crisis.* But before we retrieve it we must first know the ideal, its history, and therefore, its value.

Husserl's Three Part Examination of the Development of the Endangered Ideal

Husserl tells us that this ideal began in the Greece of Plato and Aristotle – with their ideal of philosophical "wonder." Husserl claims that ancient ideal of wonder to be much akin to his own idea of *epoché*, or the phenomenological suspension of belief. With this new attitude toward the world, one rises above the "pre-theoretical world" and becomes a detached observer of phenomena. Prior to the assumption of this attitude of wonder by Plato and Aristotle, people lived in the "natural attitude," in what Husserl calls the *Umwelt*, a world of unthinking, uncritical, everyday living (*Lebenswelt*). Since the concept of the *Lebenswelt* is not common baggage for many philosophers, a brief explanation of it is helpful.

This term has a history which has been traced first to Schleiermacher's *Erlebnis, or lived-experience* and then to Dilthey's *das Leben* (inner life). [5] Those notions were later assimilated into the phenomenological concept of the *Lebenswelt*. This term marks the general category or context of all human experience. It is the all-inclusive sphere of our finite concrete experience presupposed in any human experience whatever. This is a pre-reflective world given in brute experience and it serves as the material for our metaphysical and epistemological, cognitive articulations. This world is common to all humanity and is held to be pre-thematic and pre-cultural.

When the theoretical attitude of "wonder" was adopted by Plato and Aristotle, the *Lebenswelt* was relegated to the status of "appearance" because it was tied to a finite, changing, conventional, cultural environment of our experience. Both ancient philosophers, in their own ways, sought the experience of unchanging, "essences" and universals to provide a foundation for scientific knowledge (*episteme*). Hence, the "mere opinion" of the *Lebenswelt*, was first transcended by Plato and Aristotle as they philosophically entered the realm of a true, rigorous knowledge of the world.

However, these ancient Greeks never forgot that *episteme* was an idealization of our lived experience of the world. That was not always faithfully remembered throughout the history of Western thought. Therefore, their ideal of philosophy became more and more theoretical and less and less practical as time pressed Western philosophy onward.

It was not until the Renaissance that the classical ideal of philosophy was recovered so that theoretical understanding could again contribute to the practical world of everyday life. Nevertheless, even in this more hopeful era, the ideal underwent internal failure and eventual decomposition.

In part two of Husserl's last book, he traces the history of that failure and decomposition to Galileo, to Descartes, to Hume, and then to Kant. He begins with an analysis of Euclidean geometry that went beyond the relativities of the *Lebenswelt* by abstracting the objects of its theory from nature. Euclidean geometry also fixed a set of axioms on the basis of which deductive conclusions could be formulated. Through this idealization of the *Lebenswelt*, the limitations of perceptual knowledge were overcome and a universal, rigorous, unchanging knowledge (*episteme*) was achieved.

For Husserl Euclidean geometry was the first great intellectual revolution in Western history – the revolution upon which the *telos*, end or purpose of Western civilization is really based.

According to Husserl, Galileo inherited this ideal and science and inaugurated the second great revolution of Western intellectual history. But Galileo perverted the original ideal by forgetting that geometry was based upon an idealization of nature and was produced by the human mind. Because of Galileo, the thinking mind and the object thought about were divorced by his mathematicization of nature. This, in turn, relegated the *Lebenswelt* to a world that was so objectified that any value for human subjectivity was completely repugnant in intellectual circles of that age. It even made possible Spinoza's cosmology and metaphysics on the basis of geometry alone.

Descartes' *epoche'* went a step further than Galileo insofar as he attempted to restore subjectivity to the objectified universe as its foundation in the *ego-cogito*. For Husserl, Descartes' discovery of the *cogito* should have revealed "intentionality" to Descartes: it should have revealed that the "I" does not merely think, but always thinks *of something*. But Descartes did not make this discovery. Instead he followed in the mistaken footsteps of Galileo by regarding the "I" as a psychological reality that remains after mechanistic, mechanical nature has been subtracted from it. In short, Descartes' *epoche'* was not radical enough since he did not suspend or "bracket" the existence of the psychical "soul." This resulted in Descartes' mind-body distinction and his regarding the soul more real than the body.

According to Husserl, Descartes should have seen both mind and body as constituted by the *Ego* – an entity that transcends both mind and body and that can help us, therefore, to transcend both subjectivism and objectivism. Had Descartes seen the situation this way, he would have replaced the history of the Western ideal on its rightful, path leading to a description of a reality that contains both minds and bodies.

Instead, Descartes put the history of philosophy on a trajectory marked, on the one hand, by reductionist rationalists like Spinoza, Malebranche, Leibniz and Wolff and, on the other, by reductionist empiricists like Locke, Berkeley and Hume.

Yet, David Hume seemed to be aware of both these approaches and the bankruptcy of their reductionistic tendencies. He also showed us that science and its knowing of the world presents us with a giant enigma regarding certainty: one where either we arrive at a cheap and easy certainty of the relations of ideas or the impossibility of any certainty concerning matters of fact. By dissolving both the rationalist and empiricist sides of this enigma into skepticism, Hume came close to, but somehow failed to choose, a truly transcendental philosophy and attitude.

Kant, in answering Hume, attempted to reclaim subjectivity in his consolidation of the objective and subjective worlds. Kant claimed that the object and the subject are not separated clearly in perception and in knowledge. In other words, the world we perceive is the only one available to us. So, it makes no sense for us to seek another deeper world behind or beneath the one available to our experience. It makes no sense to speak of the internal, private career of the thing-in-itself, because that is beyond our inspection. The world as it may exist apart from our experience of it is simply unavailable to us,

Nevertheless, even then Kant bifurcates this consolidated reality into the phenomenal and the noumenal. Kant did not realize that subjectivity can not become the foundation for knowledge unless it not only has contact with the phenomena (understood by Kant as reality as it appears to us) but also with being itself (understood by Kant as the unavailable thing-in-itself).

By choosing skepticism instead of the trail Kant took later, Hume actually came closer to the life-world experience of ambiguity. Hume did not bifurcate reality but left the question open and stayed in the realm of a rigorous suspension of judgement – but a realm nonetheless hamstrung, metaphysically and epistemologically speaking.

Husserl recounts this brief history of the perversion of the ideal of Western civilization to show the critical sickness of the modern European mind – a sickness that Husserl's own transcendental phenomenology is intended to remedy by *catharsis*.

The ancient, rational ideal was perverted by physicalist objectivism and psychical subjectivism. To fetch the ideal from these perversions Husserl thought it necessary to restore our experience of the world as a pre-thematic *Lebenswelt* that is prior to its scientific idealization.

The task of part three is to see and maintain the *Lebenswelt* as the total horizon of all human experience. Through that lens, science emerges as a partial theme within the more universal *Lebenswelt*. But given the difficulties and perversions of the history of the ancient ideal, the question remains as to whether the life-world can become a likely candidate as a theme of non-reductionist and non-bifurcating reflection.

Husserl asserts that transcendental phenomenology can help here by bracketing the judgements of "scientism" and therefore can return us to the *Lebenswelt* so that we may discover the invariant stuctures within it. He claims that these structures turn out to be the same as the essential structures of idealized science but now with a welcome twist: now they are not detached essences. Husserl provides some of those structures in this part of the book. He claims that the life-world is extended in a time and space which is lived and not the detached time and space of mathematical entities. He claims that we encounter meaningful, purposeful bodies in the life-world, and not those meaningless, mechanistic bodies of physics. And he claims that the life-world contains a regularity of behavior that shows a circular, synthetic principle of causality, not a one-sided, linear causality.

For Husserl, the fact that the same structures are revealed by both the life-world and by its idealizations proves that the life-world is the foundation for all idealization. It is, therefore, pre-scientific and pre-thematic and deserves our closest attention and most rigorous study.

Thus, Husserl believes that we can be cured of our sickness and the *Crisis* can be overcome by a phenomenological reduction to the life-world. Only then can we account adequately for our human experience and can overcome reductionism, relativism, absolutism, objectivism, subjectivism, scientism, rationalism, and empiricism. According to Husserl, the life-world is the universal foundation for all the more particular sciences and the ideal of reason, consequently, may be saved.

Hence Husserl provides a phenomenological version of the ideal that is different than that of Descartes: one that would not include a "final" system of philosophy and knowledge but one that would provide an adequate foundation for the rationalization of human experience.

Merleau-Ponty's Reaction to Husserl's Overcoming of the Crisis

Merleau-Ponty saw that Husserl took his usual idealist platform from which to launch an overcoming of the crisis. He depended on a Kantian-like "philosophy of consciousness," – where truth resides in the "inner man" [3] – to help him ground his rescue of reason in the daily exchange in science and philosophy. But to Merleau-Ponty, this hardly is an adequate solution for the problematic of reason that Husserl identifies. If subjectivism and relativism provide the contours of the crisis, then locating truth conditions primarily in the subject seems an illogical way to overcome that particular crisis.

Merleau-Ponty liked Husserl's identification of the crisis and also Husserl's own gesturing toward a solution to be found in the concept of the *Lebenswelt*.[4] And again, Husserl believed that this *Lebenswelt* could provide an objective and universal ground for our scientific articulations and hypotheses. In other words, he believed that this concept could help us avoid the perversion, reductionism and sickness which go together to constitute the crisis in European sciences and in humanity in general.

As we have said, Merleau-Ponty found that to locate truth in the inner world of the subject reduced our rich lived experience to a one-sided idealism. This would only add to the celebration of the subjective, relative kinds of analyses that Husserl saw as threats to science and reason.

Yet neither did Merleau-Ponty seek a solution, as did Pierre Thevanez, in an "object-centered" ontology of the *Lebenswelt*. That proposal would slant and reduce our lived-experience in the opposite, lop-sided direction. Merleau-Ponty reckoned that if Husserl's philosophy of consciousness "flew us over" the world of lived-experience, then an equally lop-sided "object-centered" analysis would "dig us under" the *Lebenswelt*, for which philosophy is ultimately responsible to give adequate account. Besides, the "object-centered" approach would only add to the reductionist scientism of the naturalistic programs that Husserl also legitimately wished to avoid.

Consequently, Merleau-Ponty attempted to develop an authentic, multi-dimensional description of the *Lebenswelt*: one that would take us directly into the realm of our lived-experience and one that would not neglect any of its meaningful ontological features. But the question remains as to whether Merleau-Ponty succeeds where others before him, including Husserl, had failed.

Merleau-Ponty is successful in *The Visible and the Invisible* insofar as he can be seen as a twentieth-century version of Socrates, not Plato nor Aristotle, in generating the real, authentic, Socratic sense of philosophical wonder. Merleau-Ponty does not take us to a realm of eternal invariance or essences. That is not where his existential style of phenomenology leads us.

As we saw in Chapter Two, Merleau-Ponty is like Socrates insofar as his questioning and "interrogation" yield no absolutes, nor a dogmatic faith in reason. Merleau-Ponty sees the life-world as it is present to us: as a world of paradox and ambiguity and one that will always hold questions for those perceptive and insightful enough to ask them.

Clearly, then, Merleau-Ponty is important primarily because he restores philosophy to its original sense of wonder. It is a strictly Socratic wonder where the only thing we may ever know is that we don't know, one where we realize that we are fallible, one where skepticism is the only hedge against absolutistic dogmatism and the dogmatic insistence on the chaos of relativism. Merleau-Ponty truly returns us to the life-world and truly re-opens the road to inquiry. He shows us a way of remaining open to the unfolding of the manifold nature of the world.

In that last book, he also dissolves some old philosophical problems: e.g., how to account for the thickness of our lived experience without reducing it to what it is not, without contradicting it while still leaving plenty of room for *addenda.* He also dissolves the problem of other minds not by proof but by showing that intersubjectivity is presupposed by all human acts.

It is also shown by the fact that you are perceived by me as an analogous body-subject because I am the object of your subjective and meaningful gaze (thereby dissolving the subject-object distinction). He dissolves the old freedom-determinism problem by pointing out that we are free to orient our meanings within a determined and finite horizon of possibilities that are generated by our bodies and the *factical* and situational nature thereof.

Merleau-Ponty enacts a multi-faceted and adequate approach to the ontology of the life-world and fulfills Husserl's project that Husserl himself failed to complete. In short, Merleau-Ponty has helped to show us how to hedge against the idealism, relativism and dogmatism which go together to form the *Crisis* of Western civilization that Hussrl warned us about.

Consequently, Merleau-Ponty's *The Visible and the Invisible* was his authentic thrust into the *Lebenswelt qua Lebenswelt.* There, Merleau-Ponty attempts a massive, book-length phenomenological reduction which, in essence, attempts to bracket itself to reach a primordial contact with the world of lived-experience. He does that in ways presented in the sections which follow.

The Pre-Reflective Domain

Merleau-Ponty begins his last, unfinished, but most pregnant work, *The Visible and the Invisible* [7] by arguing against the absolute truth and certainty of the idealist and by arguing for a more ambiguous, pre-refelctive view of truth which, for him was consummate with the reality of the world which we inhabit:

> the naïve certitude of the world, the anticipation of an intelligible world, is as weak when it wishes to convert itself into theses as it is strong in practice. As long as we are dealing with the visible, a mass of facts comes to support it: beyond the divergence of the witness it is often easy to re-establish unity and concordance of the world. But as soon as one goes beyond the circle of *instituted* opinions, which are undivided among us as are the Madeleine or the Palais de Justice, much less thoughts and monuments of our historical landscape, as soon as one reaches the true, that is, the invisible it seems that each man inhabits his own islet, without there being transition from one to the other, and we should rather be astonished that sometimes men come to agreement about anything whatever. . . nothing is more improbable than the extrapolation that treats the universe of the truth as one world also, without fissures and without incompossibles. [8]

If there are no absolutes, if there is no universal authority, then we are presented the philosophical responsibility of discovering a purity of perception that allows us to return to *this* world, the world that we are in the midst of, the everyday lived world of human experience or *Lebenswelt.* We must behold the world that is before us and confine our analysis to that. The world of our experience is all we have to situate consciousness. The world is not some theoretical construction but a situation in which we find ourselves. But all this might lead to as many worlds as there are selves that are differently situated. How then, to account for one world that we all share and can talk with each other about? The one, commonly held world that we share turns out to be the very life-world that is before us in our experience and the one that Merleau-Ponty advises us to study.

We are responsible, then, for finding an unconditioned state where we can know about our perceptions and our interpretations and the roles they play within the whole of existence and within the scope of our lives. For Merleau-Ponty, it is only in that way that we come to any truth at all.

If we assume that our body and its senses, the apparatus of the pre-reflective, descend in epistemological status to faculties that cannot be trusted, we are then forced to abandon the physical in favor of the ideal or the conceptual. But Merleau-Ponty saw that the assumption about the body being epistemologically and metaphysically inferior to the mind was an unwise epistemological and metaphysical mistake. He wanted to avoid a false reductionism to either body or mind, because in the reality of the lived world, they cannot be separated. Instead, he speaks strongly for an irrevocable unity of body and mind:

> it is the same world that contains our bodies and our minds, provided that we understand by world not only the sum of things that fall or could fall under our eyes, but also the locus of their compossiblity, the invariable style they observe, which connects our perspectives, permits, permits transition from one to the other. [9]

Merleau-Ponty affirms the fact that, pre-reflectively speaking, we all make an initial, indubitable assumption that "there is something" to be perceived. This assumption is primordial and as true as anything will ever become for us. It is a "perceptual faith" without which we could not proceed nor live. He says:

> We see the things themselves, the world is what we see: formulae of this kind express a faith common to natural man and the philosopher – the moment he opens his eyes; they refer to a deep-seated set of mute "opinions" implicated in our lives . . . It is at the same time true that the world is *what we see* and that, nonetheless, we must learn to see it. [10]

Here Merleau-Ponty speaks about our primordial and truest contact with the world. It is our *pre-reflective* contact insofar as when we are within this experience, we pass no cognitive judgement upon that which is perceived. This experience yields one judgement only: "that there is something." But this is not a presupposition because we do not assume that there is something before we open our eyes, but only after we see that there is something. To that extent, this pre-reflective contact is pure and free of prior conditioning. It is pre-reflective to the extent that no attempt at cognitive classification has yet been made. This initial contact is cognitively innocent. And it is that fact which makes it an adequate point of departure for an authentic account of the *Lebenswelt*.

The Primordial

At the outset of our lives we possess a free and innocent attitude or comportment toward our environment. It is a pre-reflective purity of experience – a primordial, pre-cognitive, experiential truth concerning the reality of our contact with the world.

But this innocence is lost when we are *taught* to see the world – when we "learn to see it." For Merleau-Ponty, this is the beginning of the *Kulturwelt* – a world which society, philosophy, psychology, morality, religion, science, etc. would train us to see. Those social institutions retain and promote "teachers of perception" who tell us that what we saw when we opened our eyes was not truly real. Rather, those teachers claim that reality somehow lurks behind, above, or below what we can see as innocents. Therefore, those teachers of perception encourage us to search broadly for the reality of the world – a reality we already had in our innocent grasp. They tell us that the pre-reflective world is only "appearance" and "illusion" and that we must, therefore, forsake it for a rigorous and cognitive substitute.

In forsaking it we also leave behind us the primordial contact and veracity given us by our senses and bodies. We are taught that we must abandon those experiences because they are most wicked and the source of all evil. We are led, then, to bifurcate mind and body, good and evil, subject and object, *en soi* (the in-itself, objects without consciousness, brute being without consciousness, the merely physical) and *pour soi* (the for-itself, the purely mental without the physical), and appearance and reality. The innocence, truth and reality of the pre-reflective state is put aside, forgotten and/or despised just as children eventually regard their old toys.

Merleau-Ponty has his own "teachers of perception" in the forms of a fine European education, science, Husserl and Sartre. He became a fine young phenomenologist under the spell of Husserl's work and a robust existentialist with the help of Sartre. As we all do, Merleau-Ponty forgot about his pre-reflective contact with the world. Husserl taught him that the world was an idealistic, eidetic set of superstructures and Sartre taught him that the world was his own project. He traveled their proposed directions in thinking about the world, in fact, until his last and most profound work: *The Visible and the Invisible.* Only then did he begin to see through the traps of philosophy, science and the other teachers of perception. Only then could he make his break toward his true beginnings.

Perceptual Faith: A Necessary and Sufficient Condition for Contacting the World

Merleau-Ponty launches *The Visible and the Invisible* by giving us a view of the *perceptual faith* which he thought was so important, primary and primordial and which becomes a pivotal point for the remainder of his analysis. He affirms, simply, his firm belief that "we see the the things themselves, the world is what we see."[11] He claims, furthermore, that this a perceptual faith that is common to all persons.

This may seem an obvious set of remarks that could just as well have come from the naïve, natural attitude that phenomenologists warn us me must rise above. However, that set of remarks is instead the result of Merleau-Ponty's rigorous phenomenological analysis. The conclusions are the same for the naïve and the phenomenological but we are sure of the result of the phenomenological because of the rigor of the method itself. The results of the natural attitude may simply be the outcome of presupposition and dogmatism.

He moves forward to critique philosophy and science for their respective obscurities and for their refusal to take part in the world that they have placed on the examining table.[12] For Merleau-Ponty, the task of philosophy is not to endorse an impossibility or undesirability of contacting reality itself and neither is it philosophy's task to remove the philosopher from the world to gain an "objective" perch from which to observe the world's movements. Rather, just the reverse is the job of philosophy. Philosophy should be the very means for contacting the world in its most brute dimension for we who find ourselves in the midst of the world. Therefore, Merleau-Ponty concludes that philosophy is need of reform – even, perhaps especially, the philosophy of Husserl and of Sartre with whom he had learned it.

Furthermore, Merleau-Ponty maintains that in order to approach productively the questions concerning the reality of the world of perception, one must approach perception with a "clean slate," so to speak – one must approach it without presuppositions insofar as that may be possible.

Merleau-Ponty knows that for us to perceive optimally, we must become aware of our presuppositions in order to put their influence aside when we perceive. We must perceive what is before us and then report about what we have found. We must not perceive or report without really finding anything other than what we expected to find in the first place (presuppositions). Then, to perceive in this correct and productive way we must take seriously the phenomenological reduction described earlier. He says:

> Here we must presuppose nothing – neither the naïve idea of
> being in itself, therefore, nor the correlative idea of a being for
> the consciousness, of a being for man: these along with the
> being of the world, are all notions that we have to rethink with
> regard to our experience of the world. We have to reformulate
> the skeptical arguments outside of every ontological
> preconception and reformulate them precisely so as to know
> what world-being, thing-being, imaginary-being, and
> conscious being are. [13]

So things are the way they seemed to be according to our perceptual faith – our pre-reflective, primordial contact with the world. Also, incidentally, the result of the common sense, naïve attitude is validated. But, if that is true, how are we to cope with the obvious questions brought about by the illusions and mere appearances we, in fact, occasionally encounter in our lives? Merleau-Ponty claims that these "mere appearances" do not disrupt the evidence of the thing. In other words, even if we experience a moment of what is taken to be illusory perception, the moment, nevertheless, is real for us. Here, he indicates a natural process that moves us from illusion to truth: "They are phantoms and it is the real; they are pre-things and it is the thing: they vanish when we pass to normal vision and re-enter into the thing as into their daylight truth." [14]

From this he claims that perception and thinking (or, what he later calls "reflection") can be seen as mutually exclusive human activities only if one reduces experiences to theses. Granted, it is quite a difficult shift to consider thinking and perception as simultaneous acts. But this shift to simultaneity of thinking and perception is precisely what is necessary if our thinking is to be *in contact* with the world, and therefore, for our claims to say anything about *it*.

He tries to clarify what that means through an attack upon the Kantian sense of the unknowable, *ding-an-sich,* "thing in itself " or noumenal realm. Merleau-Ponty suggests that if one perceives through the presupposition that the world is mainly "in my head" as did Kant, then it is understandable to posit an unknowable neumenal realm. But this certainly would beg the question which Merleau-Ponty would yet need to answer: i.e., how, then, is it possible to contact the actual thing-in-itself?

Merleau-Ponty answers that the "thing-in-itself" which is believed to lurk behind the phenomenon which presents itself in experience may possibly be the thing just as it is seen or perceived. That which the perceptual faith allows us to contact may simply be all there is to the thing under scrutiny. But, of course, we can never demonstrate that possibility with rigorous certainty. Hence, the use of the term "faith" is not accidental. This faith, he admits, is a sort of "unjustifiable certitude." But, defending this notion, Merleau-Ponty is quick to add that the unjustifiable nature of the *perceptual faith* does not prevent us from being somehow certain about our contact with the world. He says: "the certitude, entirely irresistible as it may be remains absolutely obscure; *we can live it*, we can neither think it nor formulate it nor set it up in theses. Every attempt at elucidation brings us back to dilemmas."[15]

He clarifies this further by his remark that "the whole man is there in his infancy," or as a Buddhist would put it, "the flower is contained within the seed." Here he wished to emphasize the fluxual, gradual, unfolding yet unchanging nature of the truth concerning our contact with the things of the world. He extends this "flower-seed" idea to the human experience of perception as a whole in order to capture both the flux and fix of our pre-reflective knowledge of the world:

> it is the same world that contains our bodies and our minds,
> provided that we understand by world not only the sum of
> things that fall or could fall under our eyes, but also the locus
> of their compossibility, the invariable style they observe,
> which connects our perspectives, permits transition from one
> to another. [16]

With that he promotes the pre-reflective, unjustifiable certitude of the perceptual faith as actually being more valuable to us than the justifiable certitudes of philosophies of old. Those justifiable certainties left no room for doubts or ambiguities, became absolutes and froze our possible knowledge and experiences of the world into pre-established molds which may or may not have been caste from the things themselves. Nevertheless, these "verities" became fixed, stratified, celebrated and actually kept humans on their own rationalistic and idealistic islands and apart from the world of the things themselves. On the other hand, the unjustifiable certainties given through the pre-refelctive, perceptual faith recommend an attitude of openness, doubt and on-going interrogation, which always seeks to learn more about the ambiguities of the things in question.

Furthermore, "objective" science presupposes perceptual faith without acknowledging this presupposition. Instead the scientist tends to lie to herself in the thought that she may be able to remove herself from the world in which she is irrevocably entrenched so that she can observe it as a mere "objective" spectator. Of course, this removal is both a logical and ontological impossibility.

Science also suffers from a misunderstanding concerning the subject-object relationship. The truth of the subject-object relationship occurs in the pre-refelctive contact between "subject" and "object" – a contact that ultimately unites observer and observed. Merleau-Ponty points out that each "subject" can become an "object" for another's observation or interaction and that "objects" can become subjects that can return one's gaze. Should this be true, then where in our experience does a lived distinction between subject and object take place?

Consequently, science formulates inferences and laws from an essentially erroneous subject-object distinction and, thus, may be essentially false constructs concerning our world. Therefore, he proposes a reform wherein "'objective' and 'subjective' are recognized as two orders hastily constructed within a total experience, whose extent must be restored in all clarity." [17]

He concludes this part of his analysis of the pre-reflective, perceptual faith by returning to a consideration of the structure of the truth. Here he claims that both appearance and reality are contained within the confines of reality. Truth manifests itself gradually, and always unfolds from apparent illusions. Truth is a process of unfolding and not a singular event. Any truth, then, is not static but ultimately will be replaced by a newer and more adequate truth which, of course, will tend to reclassify the former truth as an inadequate "illusion:"

> As soon as we cease thinking of perception as the action of the
> pure physical object on the human body, and the perceived as
> the 'interior' result of this action, it seems that every
> distinction between the true and the false, between methodic
> knowledge and phantasms, between science and the
> imagination, is ruined. [18]

The Final Break with Sartre

In addition to overcoming Husserl's mistakes, Merleau-Ponty brings another "philosophy of reflection" to task: that of his friend, Jean-Paul Sartre, especially the Sartre of *Being and Nothingness*. The battle between these two men rages around the best way to speak about who and what human beings are. This is not a mere philosophical technicality but is crucial for all of us to settle personally. It is also important as a starting point for many scientific and socially scientific projects.

Merleau-Ponty reiterates the necessity for returning to the world of our primordial contact from the world of the philosophy of reflection. He encourages us to come back to the world as it is lived from the world as it is thought to be. For him, the philosophy of reflection makes its major blunder in the attempt to withdraw from or the suspension of our perceptual faith – in its retreat into a "pure" realm of concepts, propositions, reasons and arguments: "the procedure of reflection, as an appeal to 'the interior,' retreats back from the world, consigns the faith in the world to the rank of things said or *statements*."[19]

As Merleau-Ponty shows us, the withdrawal from the world is precisely the action most contrary to the one that can answer a fundamental philosophical question concerning why we believe that there is a world to begin with. The appropriate action to answer that question is a move toward the world from perceptual faith. The world is not a mere collection of thoughts, nor my "project" with which I may do what I like. The world pre-exists my thoughts about it. Our thoughts about the world are rooted in a "logic of the world" given through our perceptual faith. Our logical, conceptual order is not primordial but derivative of the activity of the perceptual faith because "it is because first I believe in the world and in the things that I believe in the order and the connection of my thoughts." [20]

Sartre's own kind of "psychological reflection" attends the states of consciousness through which we receive the world. Thus, it may seem a rudimentary, if not primordial, analysis of perception. However, according to Merleau-Ponty, psychological reflection falls prey to the same vice as any other philosophy of reflection.

Psychological reflection is mistaken in its alleged withdrawal into the world of its own ideas. If this withdrawal were possible or even desirable the world could never affect this "purified," self-conscious type of reflection – a refection "for-itself." To accomplish that retreat into consciousness-without-being would have the effect of transforming perceptual faith into signification, into "acts or attitudes of a subject that does not participate in the world." [21] Therefore, Merleau-Ponty recommends that:

> If we wish to avoid this first, irretrievable lie, it is therefore, with and through reflection the Being-subject and the Being itself that we have to conceive anew, by concentrating our attention on the horizon of the world, at the confines of the universe of reflection. For it is the horizon of the world that secretly guides us in constructions and harbors the truth of the procedures of reflection by which we pretend to reconstitute it – a first positivity of which no amount of negation or doubting could be the equivalent. [22]

Merleau-Ponty above has given hints concerning how his attack upon Sartre's philosophy of reflection and negation would flow. Sartre pronounced this "first, irretrievable lie" where he stated, in *Being and Nothingness*:

> He [man] must be able to put himself outside of being and by the same stroke weaken the structure of the being of being . . . Man's relation with being is that he can modify it. For man to put a particular existent out of circuit is to put himself out of circuit in relation to that existent. In this case he is not subject to it; he is out of reach; it can not act on him, for he has retired beyond a nothingness. [23]

That set of remarks, plus Sartre's famous distinction between the *en-soi* (the "in-itself," Being, or being-without-consciousness) and the *pour-soi* (the "for-itself," Nothingness, or consciousness-without-being) are guilty of the lie insofar as they try to remove persons from any possible contact with the world. And, as Merleau-Ponty said above, after the lie has been purchased no amount of negation is sufficient to return us to that primordial contact without which our thoughts are sheer abstractions and wishes concerning the ways in which we would like the world to be. Very simply, if we cannot be in the world then what we have to say about it will probably be false because we have not seen, touched or otherwise contacted it.

Instead, Merleau-Ponty argues that Being and Nothingness are not separate and complementary, as Sartre would have us think. Rather, they are "the obverse and reverse of the same thought." [24] He maintains that Being and Nothingness are, more precisely, synonymous terms. Whereas Sartre believed that we are separated from Being by a

Nothingness into which we must move in order to establish that only Being is, Merleau-Ponty does not believe in such a chasm between ourselves and the world. Instead, Merleau-Ponty holds that we are one with the world precisely because of that Nothingness – a literal non-existence that allows no space between self and other, subject and object, or us and the world of the things themselves.

Sartre created a strange, "ambivalent" duality that is at the same time supposed to be a synthesis between selves and the world of things. And he clearly proposes a removal of the *pour-soi* from the world. Thus, the same charge can be levied against Sartre as against the sciences. Sartre, too, wished to become "objective" as he flies to a Nothingness (and "beyond" it) and cannot affect or be affected by a world with which he has no contact. Sartre wished merely to observe. But what he forgets here is that to observe implies that "there is something" to observe and that consciousness is always intentional – consciousness is always consciousness of something – of something in the world.

Sartre's Retreat

Merleau-Ponty takes issue with Sartre at the point of Sartre's retreat into pure consciousness, into pure conception, in order that, through a dialectical negation of that consciousness, Being can be reached. Sartre was aware, of course, that to leave his investigation with the lop-sided conclusion that we are primarily minds with no essential need for bodies surely throws him back to the very claims of Descartes' dualism that Sartre intended to remedy with his work. But, given Sartre's own psychological, rather introverted make-up, he could not see his way clear to negate the consciousness he so prized in order to reach pure Being (*en-soi*). Thus, Sartre's dialectical method fell short of his goal.

Though Sartre himself could not see it until Merleau-Ponty pointed it out, Merleau-Ponty knew that Sartre never completed that last negation but felt satisfied in the role of a disembodied observer. Had Sartre completed the final negation toward Being, the negation of the negation, the way back to the world would have opened for him and established him as a self-in-situation – a situated subject, at least. But Sartre never returns to a perceptual faith. Besides, Sartre's method of contacting the world also seems extraordinarily and unnecessarily complex, futile and false:

> While a philosophy of consciousness or of reflection can
> justify the perceptual faith in the unicity of the world *only by*

reducing it to a consciousness of the identity of the world, and by making of illusion a simple privation, a philosophy of negativity entirely ratifies the pretension of the perceptual faith to open us to a world numerically one, common to all, through perspectives that are our own. [25]

Therefore, Sartre's negation is not rigorous or adequate enough for a return to the primordial perceptual faith through the negation of the negation. Instead he remains abstracted from the scene or situation, which is the very same inadequacy from which "objective" science suffers. Even in the "situations" which Sartre talks about in his most famous book, he remains an abstracted observer, the consciousness that conceptualizes the situation, removing itself, psychologically, from the situation. In fact, this psychological abstraction is so strong in Sartre that he claims not to have perceived other people in the café where he looks for his friend, Pierre, and perceives only the *absence* of Pierre instead. Merleau-Ponty saw Sartre's great difficulty:

The difficulty results from the fact that both [my constitutive consciousness and that of the other] are conceived as centrifugal acts [separate, de-centered Newtonian acts], spiritual synthesis, in which case one does not see how they could ebb back toward their source [Being]. On the contrary, it is for philosophy of the negative, the very definition of the *ipse* to adhere to a *de-facto* situation or to sustain it as its bond with Being. This exterior at the same time confirms it in its particularity, renders it visible as a partial being to the other's look, and connects it back to the whole. What was a stumbling block for the philosophy of reflection becomes, from the point of view of negativity [a proper negativity carried through to the final negation toward Being], the principle of a solution. *Everything really does come down to a matter of thinking the negative rigorously.* [26]

Since Sartre does not properly push negativity far enough to attain his own stated goal to reach toward Being, he is caught in an ambivalent situation where Being and Nothingness remain eternally separate, but actually belong together. This also puts Sartre in the throes of solipsism because of his retreat into his own consciousness and because he has refused the final negation which would have opened Being to him. Sartre never returns dialectically to the world.

Thus, Merleau-Ponty considers Sartre a "high altitude" thinker who, himself, defeats the possibility of his ever establishing his goal of adequately describing the relationship between the self and the world.

If Sartre is right about our being essentially consciousness, he also has failed to show how our interior worlds can link-up to one another. Sartre fails to answer the question about how we can justifiably retain our belief in our having one world common to us all: a world we clearly experience in our living with others. Merleau-Ponty re-emphasizes the reasons for Sartre's failure in the following passage:

> To *think* the total being – what is totally, and hence also that to which nothing is lacking, what is the whole of being – it is necessary to be outside of it, a margin of non-being; but this margin excluded from the whole prevents it from being all – the true totality should contain it too, which since it is a margin of non-being is quite impossible. [27]

From his more adequate viewpoint, Merleau-Ponty knows that we are not outside of or on the margins of being, but are obviously, undeniably, and squarely situated within it. Merleau-Ponty knows this because he knows that he is a body-subject and his body is situated in the world.

Merleau-Ponty warns Sartre about his wishful thinking here. Sartre's position of ambivalently wanting to reach being and, at the same time, being happy with consciousness alone would be an attractive position if, indeed, the concept of ambivalence were a reflection of a contact with ambivalent being – if, in short, the position was descriptive of the real situation. But, Merleau-Ponty maintains that Sartre's ambivalence is not descriptive but, rather, is a result of conscious positing, a result of abstract artistry. Merleau-Ponty argues:

> In reality, the definitions of being as what it is in all respects and without restriction, and of nothingness as what is not in any respect – this appropriation of an immediate being and of an immediate nothingness *by thought*, this intuition and this negintuition – are the abstract portrait of an experience, and it is on the terrain of experience that they must be discussed. Do they express well our contact with being, do they express it in full? [28]

Merleau-Ponty completely repudiates Sartre's description of our contact with being because, in Sartre's case, there is no contact with being. And this lack of contact is volitional and programmatic. But Merleau-Ponty is not yet finished with Sartre's philosophy.

Merleau-Ponty continues the criticism of Sartre's philosophy of who and what human beings are as he alerts us to the idea that Being and Nothingness are not reducible to the absolute fullness of Being and the absolute absence of Being. For Merleau-Ponty, if we are ever to succeed in describing our access to the things themselves, absolutistic distinctions such as Sartre's will not help. He says that: "This distinction, like the others, has to be reconsidered and is not reducible to that between the full and the void."[29]

Sartre's High Altitude Philosophy

An absolutist, purist, disengaged, high-altitude philosophy like Sartre's prevents any contact with being whatsoever. Merleau-Ponty jabs at Sartre as he remarks: "High places attract those who wish to look over the world with an eagle's-eye view. Vision ceases to be solipsistic only up close." [30] In other words, Merleau-Ponty feels that Sartre must be quite uncomfortable with the facticity of existing as a mere human being – as only a part of Being-as-a-whole. Evidently Sartre would rather become absolute, pure Being, or at least the reverse: absolute, pure consciousness. Merleau-Ponty realizes the futility and *hubris* of such a desire. Merleau-Ponty, himself, is content with being "on equal footing with those who, enclosed within those walls [of Notre Dame, as opposed to those, like Sartre, who are perched atop its towers] there minutely pursue incomprehensible tasks." [31]

For Merleau-Ponty, the world of the things themselves is not one of cleanly drawn "either-or" distinctions, and not one that permits black *or* white, Being *or* Nothingness. On the contrary, what is given in our perceptual faith are many finite and blending shades of *both* Being *and* Nothingness simultaneously. The world of the things themselves is much more ambiguous than Sartre would allow. It falls to us as our humble, but "incomprehensible task" to somehow account for these many individual shadings and nuances that are all on the same footing, equal even to us.

For instance, the "other" need not be an empty, alienating "hell" as Sartre once classified her. According to Merleau-Ponty, the "other" is a brother or sister being belonging to the same order of being that I do. The "other" can help to re-install being back into consciousness (which Sartre emptied through his cavalier negation) by throwing her conscious gaze upon me. This gaze is not the empty look of a robot or mindless creature but rather comes from the riveting eyes of another perceptive, conscious and judging human subject. By gazing at me she shows that she is not empty of consciousness and I am not full of consciousness to the point of monopolizing it. This simple interaction with the "other" reveals that I too am an "object" for the conscious perception of another and that she is a "subject" consciously perceiving. It reveals, ultimately, that we both represent ambiguous shades and amounts of *both* Being *and* Nothingness.

Both the "other" and I interact within an atmosphere that has limits and contours. We do not and cannot transcend these limits in order to interact, as Sartre would have us believe. The contact is made within and through these limits:

> The involvement of men in the world and of men in one another, even if it can be brought about only by means of *perception*s and acts, is transversal with respect to the spatial and temporal multiplicity of the actual. But this must not lead us into the inverse error, which would be to treat this order of involvement as a transcendental, intemporal order. [32]

Once again and always, we must take the world and our true situation into account while we construct our philosophies. We must be open to a real, primordial position of being "in the world" and must avoid trying to "shoe-horn" the world into our preferred ideas about it. We must bravely continue to interrogate this ambiguous, elusive realm given by the perceptual faith and not fearfully retire to cower in our own, more comfortable, idealistic or transcendental desires. We must reconsider and interrogate everything as it is, not as it may be more convenient and pleasing for us. We need, as Merleau-Ponty points-out, a more authentic and robust form of the Cartesian doubt. Merleau-Ponty radically states the conditions for this kind of doubt: "Oh Dialectic! says the philosopher, when he comes to the realization that perhaps the true philosopher flouts philosophy." [33]

Merleau-Ponty realized that a proper use of the dialectic takes the situational along with it as a valued friend. In using the dialectic well, one does not reject individual, real situations as not being pure enough for philosophical consideration. One does not artfully and artificially restrict plurality and ambiguity to that which can be processed with familiar and facile concepts of one's aesthetic preference.

If we are to answer the fundamental question of what it is to be in this world, we must first bold enough to ask it authentically. By facing the world and its questions with preconceptions we do not really ask anything. Tragically and simply, by so articulating the world we assert according to our pleasures and delights. Instead, we must be willing to ask anew and renounce our secret conceptual manipulations of what we would like the world to be. To reach the world of the things themselves, we must go nakedly into the very depths of the unknown, ambiguous and mysterious to question brute being about the brute. As Merleau-

Ponty puts it: "Philosophy is the perceptual; faith questioning itself about itself." [34]

Thus ends Merleau-Ponty's critique of Sartre's philosophy that marks his final break with Sartre. But before Merleau-Ponty can become himself as a philosopher, he must clear the ground and make a clean break with another of his "teachers of perception," Edmund Husserl.

The Final Break with Husserl

In his chapter entitled "Interrogation and Intuition," Merleau-Ponty shows the difficulties inherent in philosophies such as Husserl's philosophy of "essence." Once again, the old problem of "detachment from the world" raises its head as the major problem in the philosophy of essence. And this time, it takes its shape from Husserl's bifurcation of essence and fact. Husserl's eidetic method removes essence from fact by searching the pre-reflective presentation of the thing-in-itself for a higher, less ambiguous meaning. In so doing, Husserl "soars over" the situational and, thus, joins the ranks of those who would make a mere appearance of our real, brute world. Merleau-Ponty puts it this way:

> A pure essence which would not be at all contaminated and confused with facts could result only from an attempt at total variation. It would require a spectator himself without secrets, without latency, if we are to be certain that nothing be surreptitiously introduced into it. In order to really reduce an experience to its essence, we should have to achieve a distance from it that would put it entirely under our gaze, with all the implications of sensoriality or thought that come into play in it and bring ourselves wholly to the transparency of the imaginary, think it without the support of any ground, in short withdraw to the bottom of nothingness. Only then could we know what moments positively make up the being of this experience. *But would this still be an experience, since I would be soaring over it?* [35]

On the contrary, Merleau-Ponty understood that essence (an unchanging, eternal, defining idea available only to the mind) and fact (an objective world available only to our senses) are one and the same thing and are only the flip-side of one another, especially as given through our perceptual faith. Hence, Husserl's distinction between fact and essence turns out to be just as false as that between subject and object and Being and Nothingness. The duality of fact and essence is simply unreal for Merleau-Ponty and he can no longer find a way to reinterpret Husserl to make him sound more authentic and "true to life." As he says:

> Fact and essence can no longer be distinguished, not because, mixed up in our experience, they in their purity would be inaccessible and would subsist as a limit – ideas beyond our experience, but because – Being no longer *before me*, but surrounding me in a sense of traversing me, and my vision of Being not forming itself from elsewhere, *but from the midst of Being* – the alleged facts, the spatio-temporal individuals, are from the first mounted on the axes, the pivots, the dimensions, *the generality of my body, and the ideas are therefore already encrusted in its joints.* [36]

That last phrase of the quotation in italics above illuminates Merleau-Ponty's own cleared pathway to his formulation of "interrogation," the mind-body relationship, and other new findings. Merleau-Ponty has now made his break with the inadequate philosophies and presuppositions of his old "teachers of perception," and is ready to examine authentically his contact with the world from within his situation in the world – even with all of its ambiguities, shadows, shades, nuances and brute facts.

Merleau-Ponty's Brave Analysis: The Intertwining – The Chiasm

In his last full chapter of the book, "The Intertwining – The Chiasm," Merleau-Ponty begins his own work, perhaps for the very first time. It is unfortunate, indeed, that it was to be his last work as well. There are no maps for this kind of analysis. Yet, he goes bravely toward the meaning of his perceptual faith – and he goes alone. He has unconditioned himself and moves into the meaning of the brute *qua* brute.

In this chapter, Merleau-Ponty finds it useful for his phenomenological description to formulate the idea of "reversibility." To show an example of what he means, he considers the experience of touching. As the hand is felt from both within and from without, as the toucher is touched by that which is touched, so fall away all the former distinctions of his past. Gone now are subject-object distinctions,

62

essence-fact distinctions and distinctions concerning Being and Nothingness. Gone too are the false certainties and verities concerning whom is acting upon what. Here the philosopher "in the world" is forcefully revealed and re-emphasized. The philosopher does not look above or below the appearances for his clues about his relationship to them nor for his concepts concerning the nature of the things themselves. The things speak quite loudly for themselves when we stay in the world. He says: " He who looks must not himself be foreign to the world he looks at." [37]

The Primordial Flesh

Merleau-Ponty reminds us of something we already know without question through our lived experience: that the body is not separate from the mind. For instance, the reader would not be reading this work if it were not for the fact that I consciously command my body to move in specific ways so that I may enter these words into a word processor through tapping them out on this keyboard. Perhaps this seems obvious to the non-professional philosopher or the person on the street. Nevertheless, in the professional field of philosophy Merleau-Ponty's idea of a body-subject is revolutionary, especially given the hold that Descartes' mind-body dualism has had on the history of philosophy.

Merleau-Ponty arrives at this view by being aware of his presuppositions, laying them aside insofar as he can and, through his perceptual faith, by returning to a real, lived, everyday experience of our world. Hence, by breaking with his philosophically conditioned perception and by phenomenologically retraining his perception and turning it upon what we actually experience, he can say boldly that the body is our primordial means of opening up the world to our consciousness. Our *flesh* is that irrevocable combination and composite of body and mind, intertwined into that being whom we *live,* and through which we communicate and interact with the real world of the things themselves.

This is possible because our *flesh* is part of the *flesh* of the world – part of the logic and substance of the world – part of the "prose of the world." The *flesh* covers both idea and body, inner and outer, Being and Nothingness, subject and object, essence and fact: all are part of the *flesh of the world.*

The flesh is not merely an outer skin tied across our bones to keep our organs internal to us. The flesh, in Merleau-Ponty's use, does not end at the extremities of our bodies, nor does it begin with those extremities. The flesh might be explained best by drawing a parallel between the flesh and the contention that, though it may appear that there is such a thing as vacant and empty space between objects, the universe is really full with no empty space at all. The apparent empty space is filled with sub-particles, radio waves and all sorts of other imperceivable matter. From his new perspective, Merleau-Ponty says the universe is one great mass of *flesh*.

Therefore, all Being is part of the same flesh. This provides an interesting juncture in the analysis. It would seem that the only Being left to interrogate is we, ourselves – giving a brand new dimension to the ancient Greek credo: *know thyself*! But what can the brute being say about the brute being, especially to the brute being?

The answer can be silence. Only nothing is the appropriate answer, for nothing need be said. Are we not one and identical with ourselves? And do we not know that? If so, we know all that need be known by merely being. Yet, this is the most profound mystery of them all: ourselves. It represents a strange paradox, but a paradox involving all of Being. As Merleau-Ponty says:

> Since the total invisible is always behind, or after, or between the aspects we see of it, there is access to it only through an experience which like it, is wholly outside of itself. It is thus, and not as the bearer of an knowing subject, that our body commands the visible for us, but it does not explain it, does not clarify it, it only concentrates the mystery of its scattered visibility; and it is *indeed a paradox of Being*, not of man, that we are dealing with here.[38]

From the passage above, it is clear that the subject-object pattern in thinking is no longer pertinent for Merleau-Ponty and the new pattern that he prefers takes some shifting of gears. Now, his is a paradoxical way of thinking and of perceiving: one that more closely matches the ambiguity of the world.

In brief, if we want to be accurate, we have no choice but to think in paradoxical ways about our ambiguous and paradoxical world of experience. So Merleau-Ponty is not disillusioned by paradoxes coming from this long analysis, because they represent necessary adjustments of our brave new perspective on the pre-reflective brute contact with the being of the world given by the perceptual faith. They represent a "clearing" or an "horizon" against which is reckoned the distance and the nearness of the things themselves:

> No more than the sky or the earth is the horizon a collection of things held together, or a class name, or a logical possibility of conception, or a system of 'potentiality of consciousness': it is

a new type of being, a being by porosity, pregancy, or generality, and he before whom the horizon opens is caught up, included within it. His body and the distances participate in one and the same corporeity or visibility in general, which reigns between them and it, and even beyond the horizon, beneath the skin unto the depths of being. [39]

Merleau-Ponty would have given us more of a complete description of this new pattern of thinking, but was cut off from it by his death. In the incomplete chapter called "Pre-objective Being: The Solipsist World," his life's work comes to an abrupt end. He tells us in reminder and in parting:

> Let us therefore consider ourselves installed among the multitude of things, living beings, symbols, instruments, and men, and let us try to form notions that would enable us to comprehend what happens to us there. Our first truth – which prejudges nothing and cannot be contested – will be that there is presence, that 'something' is there, that 'someone' is there.[40]

With that, Merleau-Ponty carries us straightforwardly and bravely into the *Lebenswelt*, authentically overcomes many crises of philosophy, and sends us in the direction of the things themselves – as they and we become the flesh of the world.

[1] Matthieu Casalis, "Merleau-Ponty's Philosophical Itinerary: From Phenomenology to Onto-Semiology," in *The Southwestern Journal of Philosophy*, February, 1975, p. 63.

[2] Edmund Husserl, *The Crisis of European Sciences and Transcendental Phenomenology*, Evanston: Northwestern University Press, 1970.

[5] See Howard N. Tuttle, *Wilhelm Dilthey's Philosophy of Historical Understanding: A Critical Analysis*, Leiden: E. J. Brill, 1969, pp. 12-20.

[3] See especially the last paragraph of Husserl's *Cartesian Meditations*, p. 157, where he writes:

> The Delphic motto, 'Know thyself!' has gained a new signification. Positive science is a science lost in the world by epoche, in order to regain it by a universal self-examination. 'Do not wish to go out,' says Augustine, 'go back into yourself; truth dwells in the inner man.'

[4] Husserl, *The Crisis of European Sciences and Transcendental Phenomenology*, pp. 173-174.

[7] Maurice Merleau-Ponty, *The Visible and the Invisible*, Evanston: Northwestern University Press, 1968.

[8] *Ibid.*, pp. 13-14.

[9] *Ibid.*, pp. 13.

[10] *Ibid.*, pp. 3-4.

[11] *Ibid.*, p. 3.

[12] For a close similarity with Merleau-Ponty's critique here, see also John Dewey's "spectator view of knowledge" as seen in his *Quest for Certainty: A Study of the Relation of Knowledge and Action*, New York: Minton, Balch and Company, 1929, pp. 22-23 and his *Art as Experience*, New York: Minton, Balch and Company, 1934, pp. 13-17, where Dewey says what could just as well come from the pen of Merleau-Ponty:

> Life goes on in an environment; not merely *in* it but because of it . . . The contrast of lack and fullness, of struggle and achievement, of adjustment after consummated irregularity, form the drama in which action, feeling, and meaning are one. The outcome is balance and counterbalance. They express power that is intense because measured through overcoming resistance. Environing objects avail and counteravail . . . The

moment of passage from disturbance into harmony is that of intensest life.

[13] Merleau-Ponty, *The Visible and the Invisible*, p. 7.

[14] *Ibid.*, p. 7.

[15] *Ibid.*, p. 11.

[16] *Ibid.*, p. 13.

[17] *Ibid.*, p. 20.

[18] *Ibid.*, p. 26.

[19] *Ibid.*, p. 50.

[20] *Ibid.*, pp. 50-51.

[21] *Ibid.*, p. 51.

[22] *Ibid.*, p. 51.

[23] Jean-Paul Sartre, *Being and Nothingness*, New York: Washington Square Press, 1953, pp. 59-60.

[24] Merleau-Ponty, *The Visible and the Invisible*, p. 52.

[25] *Ibid.*, p. 62.

[26] *Ibid.*, p. 62-63. Brackets mine.

[27] *Ibid.*, p. 74.

[28] *Ibid.*, p. 75.

[29] *Ibid.*, p. 77.

[30] *Ibid.*, p. 78.

[31] *Ibid.*, p. 34.

[32] *Ibid.*, p. 85.

[33] *Ibid.*, p. 93.

[34] *Ibid.*, p. 103.

[35] *Ibid.*, p. 111.

[36] *Ibid.*, p. 114.

[37] *Ibid.*, p. 134.

[38] *Ibid.*, p. 136.

[39] *Ibid.*, p. 149.

[40] *Ibid.*, p. 160.

4

Epilogue: Where Merleau-Ponty Pointed

There has been some speculation that Merleau-Ponty would have finished *The Visible and the Invisible* in the direction he took in an article called "The Eye and the Mind,"[1] and in *The Prose of the World*.[2] In *The Visible and the Invisible* he analogously applied his account of our perception of 'visible' objects to his advice concerning how to talk authentically about the 'invisible' portion of our experiences. He took that avenue also in the other works mentioned above that can give us some hint as to the direction he would have taken had he lived long enough to complete his philosophical journey.

The Prose of the World

In *The Prose of the World*, also an unfinished work at the time of his death, Merleau-Ponty makes a central claim. He claims that the speech of common language plays a special role in our sharing of the world, a role very like that of the body in perception. "Speaking language" can yield common meanings which pre-exist us and to which we may add our own nuance. As long as it is generated full well from the midst of the flesh, this "becoming of language," this on-going speaking of the truth concerning our experience occurs within a culture with a common language. Merleau-Ponty describes this becoming of language through our on-going common speech about our brute contact with the world:

> Just as our common membership in the same world
> presupposes that my experience, insofar as it is original,
> should be the experience of being, so our membership in a
> common language or even a common universe of language

presupposes a primordial relation between me and my speech, which gives it the value of a dimension of being in which I can participate. Through this relation, the other myself can become other and can become myself in a much more radical sense. The common language which we speak is something like the anonymous corporeality which we share with other organisms. [3]

Just as our bodies enable and sustain our contact and interactions with the world of the things themselves, so too does the language enable and sustain our living in a world of public, shared, and lived truths. *The Prose of the World*, then, is a work that points in the direction of discussions concerning the "becoming of language" and the intersubjectivity presupposed by the existence and use of a common language – all of which help us share our contact with the pre-reflective, brute Being of the world.

It is keenly important for Merleau-Ponty that this sharing is *spoken*. It is the spoken word that is alive and forceful. It delivers meanings unavailable in written communication. In fact, Merleau-Ponty once commented that one should *sing* the meanings of her existence. Here he means *sing* in the more ancient meaning of that term, when poets would *sing* about the heroic virtues of Ulysses and Hector, giving the spoken word a more musical, poetic, aesthetic and more powerfully evocative impact upon the audience. This impact is vivacious and lively and closer to the experience that the singer is trying to share and evoke in the hearer. It is more primordial and pre-reflectively known.

The Eye and Mind

The article, "Eye and Mind" appears in *The Primacy of Perception* and launches us in a similar, yet more interesting direction of a discussion concerning painting. Merleau-Ponty begins the piece by saying: "What I am trying to translate to you is more mysterious; it is entwined in the very roots of being, in the impalpable source of sensations. (J. Gasquet, *Cézanne*)." [4]

He moves ahead to say many of the things already mentioned above concerning his critique of science's looking at the things from above, etc., thereby making science inadequate for the task of articulating our intimate contact with the world of the things given by the perceptual faith. But then Merleau-Ponty had the insight to turn to art as a discipline that might better accommodate an articulation of that contact:

> But art, especially painting draws upon this fabric of brute meaning which activism [or operationalism – *Trans.*] would prefer to ignore. Art and only art does so in full innocence. From the writer and the philosopher, in contrast, we want opinions and advice. We will not allow them to hold the world suspended. We want them to take a stand; they cannot waive the responsibilities of men who speak. Music, at the other extreme, is too far beyond the world and the designatable to depict anything but certain outline of Being – its ebb and flow, its growth, its upheavals, its turbulence. Only the painter is entitled to look at everything without being obliged to appraise what he sees. For the painter, we might say, the watchwords of knowledge and action lose their meaning and force . . . Strong or frail in life, he is incontestably sovereign in his own rumination of the world. With no other technique than what his eyes and hands discover in seeing and painting, he persists in drawing from this world, with its din of history's glories and scandals, *canvases* which will hardly add to the angers or the hopes of man – and no one complains. [5]

Artists like Cézanne painted his phenomenological experience of what he actually saw and felt pre-reflectively in his visual field. But we must remember that not all kinds of painting can thus capture the mystery and ambiguity of our brute contact with world. Only a painter like Cézanne can do that kind of work. The classical paintings of the Renaissance or the realists, on the other hand, tried to capture objects as seen clinically, as they are in themselves, as they are objectively or noumenally. But they did not capture the pre-refelctive feelings of those who had those perceptions of those objects. They did not contain our lived experience of those moments of perception. Insofar as that is true of Renaissance paintings, they are less than authentic expressions of our contact with the world.

In an earlier work (1948), titled "Cézanne's Doubt," Merleau-Ponty refers to the kind of painting that *is* up to the task of capturing real-life, brute contact with the world of things themselves – with all of its uncertainties, nuances and ambiguity:

> It is clear from his conversations with Emile Bernard that Cézanne was always seeking to avoid the ready-made alternatives suggested to him: sensations versus judgment; the

painter who sees against the painter who thinks; nature versus composition; primitivism as opposed to tradition . . . Rather than apply to his work dichotomies more appropriate to those who sustain traditions than to those men, philosophers or painters, who initiate these traditions, he preferred to search for the true meaning of painting, which is to continually question tradition. Cézanne did not think he had to choose between feeling and thought, between order and chaos. He did not want to separate the stable things which we see and the shifting way in which they appear; he wanted to depict matter as it takes on form, the birth of order through spontaneous organization . . . Cezanne wanted to paint this primordial world, and his pictures therefore seem to show nature pure. [6]

Cézanne tried to capture the unfolding of the world through the use of his perceptual faith. He tired to show how the world of the things themselves eventually emerge distinctly from a seemingly chaotic assembly of indirect and vague shapes and colors. He tried to show the things as they emerge from a flow of being into a recognizable emerging order just as they do in our actual vision. Hence, Cézanne's painting is tied directly to the elements and movements of our *Lebenswelt*, just as all of our disciplines ought to be. To finish this speculative section concerning where Merleau-Ponty might have taken us, had he lived long enough to complete the articulation of his vision, I turn to a passage from "Eye and Mind" that encases that vision. It shows why painting is his clue for how to articulate authentically the life-world, and brings us back to the idea of perceptual faith with which he began *The Visible and the Invisible*:

The Painter 'takes his body with him,' says Valéry. Indeed we cannot imagine how a *mind* could paint. It is by lending his body to the world that the artist changes the world into paintings. To understand these transubstantiations we must go back to the working, actual body – not the body as a chunk of space or a bundle of functions but that body which is an intertwining of vision and movement. . . Visible and mobile, my body is a thing among things; it is caught in the fabric of the world, and its cohesion is that of a thing. But because it moves itself and sees, it holds things in a circle around itself; they are incrusted into its flesh, they are part of its full definition; the world is made of the same stuff as the body. This way of turning things around, these antinomies, are different ways of saying that vision happens among, or is caught in, things – in that place where something visible undertakes to see, becomes visible for itself by virtue of the sight of things; in that place where there persists, like the mother water in crystal, the undividedness of the sensing and the sensed. [7]

Merleau-Ponty knows that we are in the world and our songs concerning that experience must be sung in a way that makes it clear that we, as body-subjects, are always and irrevocably situated *here* in the midst of the things themselves. That is who and what we are and what there is to know.

Conclusion

Merleau-Ponty scouted a path that arrives at a crossroad. Either we meet the ambiguity, paradoxes and flux of the world and understand and articulate our experiences of them by being silent – silent in the knowledge that meaning escapes our traditional means of capturing it. Or we can meet the flux and becoming artistically and authentically by articulating our meanings through art, poetry, myth and analogy – through indirect means. Since Merleau-Ponty has shown us that it is our politically duty to engage the world not in silence but by articulating accurately the experiences we live through, we must become artists who sing the songs of our lives and of our world.

For that kind of creative project, straight scientific and philosophical prose are inappropriate, since they tend to stratify and "straightjacket" our brute encounter with the world. Our traditional language of record takes beings in motion only to freeze and reify them. Objectification and stratification of this sort is artificial and false because, in describing a rather wild *becoming*, this smooth and convenient passage of out minds and our philosophical language domesticates it as *being*. At that point, meaning is no longer to be found where we live situated in our spatio-temporal life-world. Rather, it is falsely exiled to a Platonic realm of static, mental forms. This is not the meaning we humans experience in the world. The upshot of all this is that, after understanding Merleau-Ponty, we should be somewhat uncomfortable when we speak directly, boldly but falsely about the world of the things themselves, as if we had its meaning by a quick and easy handle.

We should only "gesture' toward our pre-reflective contact with the brute world through indirect means – through stories, myths, analogies and parables, paintings, poetry and songs. Like Cézanne, we must learn to *paint* our meanings from and on the canvas of the *Lebenswelt*.

The utility of these modes of expression is not new to thinkers who have tried to say something that is very difficult, but important to say. But these modes of expression are not all that welcome or valued in our technocratic, glib and facile slice of time.

Merleau-Ponty's writings are his "song of becoming," and are his most effective and authentic ways of capturing what he knows about the flesh of the world, a flesh in which we live and in which we die. His writings are the media through which he carried meaningful human discourse a few steps forward toward a rigorous, true and authentic account of our selves and the experience of our world.

Maurice Merleau-Ponty is important for us all to read, to hear, to understand, to reflect upon and to criticize from our own viewpoints. Like Socrates, he reopens the world of our experience to authentic wonder and interrogation. He gives us a point of departure to become truly engaged thinkers and actors. With that, he has given us quite a gift: he has made alive again the possibility of new and crucial philosophical discoveries and the option of real human community.

[1] See footnote number one, in Maurice Merleau-Ponty's *Primacy of Perception*, Evanston: Northwestern University Press, 1964, p. 159, where the translator of "Eye and Mind," Carleton Dallery says:

> According to Professor Claude Lefort, "L'Oeil et l'esprit" is a preliminary statement of ideas that were developed in the second part of the book Merleau-Ponty was writing at the time of his death – *Le visible et l'invisible*.

[2] Maurice Merleau-Ponty, *The Prose of the World*, Evanston: Northwestern University Press, 1973.

[3] *Ibid.*, p. 140.

[4] Maurice Merleau-Ponty, "Eye and Mind," *The Primacy of Perception*, Evanston: Northwestern University Press, 1964, p. 159.

[5] *Ibid.*, p. 161.

[6] Maurice Merleau-Ponty, "Cézanne's Doubt," *Sense and Non-Sense*, Evanston: Northwestern University Press, 1964, p. p. 13.

[7] Merleau-Ponty, "Eye and Mind," p. 162.

Selected Bibliography

Selected Works by Merleau-Ponty

Merleau-Ponty, Maurice, *The Structure of Behavior*, Boston: Beacon Press, 1963.

Merleau-Ponty, Maurice, *Phenomenology of Perception*, New York: Humanities Press, 1962.

Merleau-Ponty, Maurice, *In Praise of Philosophy*, Evanston: Northwestern University Press, 1963.

Merleau-Ponty, Maurice, *Sense and Non-Sense*, Evanston: Northwestern University Press, 1964.

Merleau-Ponty, Maurice, *The Primacy of Perception*, Evanston: Northwestern University Press, 1964.

Merleau-Ponty, Maurice, *Signs*, Evanston: Northwestern University Press, 1964.

Merleau-Ponty, Maurice, *The Visible and the Invisible*, Evanston: Northwestern University Press, 1968.

Merleau-Ponty, Maurice, *Humanism and Terror*, Boston: Beacon Press, 1969.

Merleau-Ponty, Maurice, *Themes from the Lectures at the College de France 1952-1960*, Evanston: Northwestern University Press, 1970.

Merleau-Ponty, Maurice, *Consciousness and the Acquisition of Language*, Evanston: Northwestern University Press, 1973.

Merleau-Ponty, Maurice, *The Prose of the World*, Evanston: Northwestern University Press, 1973.

Merleau-Ponty, Maurice, *Adventures of the Dialectic*, London: Heineman, 1974.

Merleau-Ponty, Maurice, *Texts and Dialogues: Contemporary Studies in Philosophy and the Human Sciences*, edited by Silverman and Barry, New Jersey: Humanities Press, 1992.

Selected Works

On Merleau-Ponty's Philosophy

Books

Archard, D., Marxism and Existentialism, Belfast: Blackstaff Press, 1980.

Bannan, John F., *The Philosophy of Merleau-Ponty*, New York: Harcourt, Brace & World, Inc., 1967.

Edie, James M., *Merleau-Ponty's Philosophy of Language: Structuralism and Dialectics*, Washington, D.C.: University Press of America, 1987.

Johnson, Mark, *The Body in the Mind*, Chicago: University of Chicago Press, 1987.

Kwant, Remey C., *From Phenomenolgy to Metaphysics: An Inquiry into the Last Period of Merleau-Ponty's Philosophical Life*, Pittsburgh, Pa.: Duquesne University Press, 1966.

Kwant, Remey C., *The Phenomenolgical Philosophy of Merleau-Ponty*, Pittsburgh, Pa.: Duquesne University Press, 1963.

Selected Bibliography

Lakoff, George, and Johnson, Mark, *Philosophy in the Flesh: The Embodied Mind and Its Challenge to Western Thought*, New York: Basic Books, 1999.

Langan, Thomas, *Merleau-Ponty's Critique of Reason*, New Haven: Yale University Press, 1966.

Madison, G., *The Phenomenology of Merleau-Ponty*, Athens, Ohio: Ohio University Press, 1981.

Mallin, Samuel B., *Merleau-Ponty's Philosophy*, New Haven: Yale University Press, 1979.

O'Neill, J., *Perception, Expression and History*, Evanston: Northwestern University Press, 1970.

Articles

Abram, David, "Merleau-Ponty and the Voice of the Earth," *Environmental Ethics*, v. 10, Summer 1988, p. 101.

Ashbaugh, Anne F., "The Fool in the Farce: Merleau-Ponty's 'Philosophy of,' " *Philosophy Today*, v. 27, Winter 1983, p. 326.

Barry, J., "The Textual Body: Incorporating Writing and Flesh," *Philosophy Today*, v. 30, Spring 1986, p. 16.

Barta-Smith, Nancy A., "When Time is not a River: Landscape, Memory, History, and Merleau-Ponty," *International Philosophical Quarterly*, Dec. 1997, v. 37, n 4, p. 423

Bourgeois, Patrick L., "The Epistemic Dimensions of Existential Phenomenolgy," *Philosophy Today*, v. 30, Spring 1986, p. 43.

Bourgeois, Patrick L., and Rosenthal, Sandra B., "Role Taking, Corporeal Intersubjectivity, and Self: Mead and Merleau-Ponty," *Philosophy Today*, v. 34, Summer 1990, p. 117.

Casalis, Matthieu, "Merleau-Ponty's Philosophical Itinerary: From Phenomenology to Onto-Semiology," *The Southwestern Journal of Philosophy*, February, 1975.

Cohen Richard A., "Merleau-Ponty, The Flesh and Foucault, *Philosophy Today*, v. 28, Winter 1984, p. 329.

Compton, John J., "Merleau-Ponty's Metaphorical Philosophy," *Research in Phenomenology*, v. 23, 1993, p. 221.

Duffy, Jean, "Claude Simon, Merleau-Ponty and Perception," *French Studies*, v. 46, January 1992, p. 33.

Fielding, Helen, "Depth of Embodiment: Spatial and Temporal Bodies in Foucault and Merleau-Ponty," *Philosophy Today*, v. 43, no. 1, Spring 1999, p. 73.

Foti, Veronique, "On Truth/Untruth in Heidegger and Merleau-Ponty," *Research in Phenomenology*, v. 13, 1983, p. 185.

Gallagher, Shaun, "The Lived Body and Environment," *Research in Phenomenology*, v. 16, 1986, p. 139.

Garner, Stanton B., "'Still Living Flesh': Beckett, Merleau-Ponty, and the Phenomenological Body," *Theatre Journal*, v. 45, December 1993, p. 443.

Gill, Jerry H., "Merleau-Ponty Metaphor, and Philosophy," *Philosophy Today*, v. 34, Spring 1990, p. 49.

Hamrick, William S., "Merleau-Ponty's View of Creativity and its Philosophical Consequences," *International Philosophical Quarterly*, v. 34, December 1994, p. 401.

Hurst, William J., "Merleau-Ponty's Ontological Quest," *International Philosophical Quarterly*, v. 34, September, 1994, p. 335.

Johnson, Galen A., "Merleau-Ponty's Early Aesthetics of Historical Being: The Case of Cezanne," *Research in Phenomenolgy*, v. 17, 1987, p. 211.

Levin, David Michael, "Singing the World: Merleau-Ponty's Phenomenolgy of Language," *Philosophy Today*, v. 42, no. 3, Fall 1998, p. 319.

Lowry, Atherton C., "Condemned to Time: The Limits of Merleau-Ponty's Quest for Being," *International Philosophical Quarterly*, v. 31, September 1991, p. 319.

Mancini, Sandro, and Tomarchio, John, "Merleau-Ponty's Phenomenology as a Dialectical Philosophy of Expression," *International Philosophical Quarterly*, Dec. 1996, v 36, n4, p. 389.

Muldoon, Mark, "Time, Self, and Meaning in the Works of Henri Bergson, Maurice Merleau-Ponty, and Paul Ricoeur," *Philosophy Today*, 35, no. 3-4, Fall 1991, p. 254.

Nagel, Christopher, "Hegelianism in Merleau-Ponty's Philosophy of History," *Philosophy Today*, v. 41, Summer 1997, p. 288.

Olkowski-Laetz, Dorothea, "Merleau-Ponty: The Demand for Mystery in Language," *Philosophy Today*, v. 31, Winter 1987, p. 352.

Olson, Carl, "The Human Body as a Boundary Symbol: A Comparison of Merleau-Ponty and Dogen," *Philosophy East and West*, v. 36, April 1986, p. 107.

Prendeville, Brendan, "Psychophysical Space and the Space of Exchange," *Art History*, Sept. 1999, v. 22, I 3, p. 331.

Seigel, Jerrold, "A Unique Way of Existing: Merleau-Ponty and the Subject," *Journal Of the History of Philosophy*, v. 29, July 1991, p. 455.

Stenstad, Gail, "Merleau-Ponty's Logos: The Sens-ing of Flesh," *Philosophy Today*, v. 37, Spring 1993, p. 52.

Stewart, Jon, "Merleau-Ponty's Cristicism of Sartre's Theory of Freedom," *Philosophy Today*, v. 39, Fall 1995, p. 311.

Tagore, Saranindranath, "The Echo of Silence: Toward a Reconstruction of Merleau-Ponty's Philosophy of History," *International Philosophical Quarterly*, v. 31, December 1991, p. 427.

Toadvine, Theodore A., "The Art of Doubting: Merleau-Ponty and Cezanne," *Philosophy Today*, Winter 1997, v. 41, n1, p. 545.

Tuedio, James, "Merleau-Ponty's Refinement of Husserl," *Philosophy Today*, v. 29, Summer 1985, p. 99.

Waldenfels, Bernard, "Verite a faire: Merleau-Ponty's Question Concerning Truth," *Philosophy Today*, v. 35, Summer 1991, p. 185.

Watson, Stephen, "Cancellations: Notes on Merleau-Ponty's Standing Between Hegel and Husserl," *Research in Phenomenolgy*, v. 17, 1987, p. 191.

Watson, Stephen, "Merleau-Ponty and Foucault: Deaestheticization of the Work of Art," *Philosophy Today*, v. 28, Summer 1984, p. 148.

Weiner, Scott E., "'Inhabiting' in the Phenomenology of Perception," *Philosophy Today*, v. 34, Winter 1990, p. 342.

Weiss, Allen S., "Merleau-Ponty's Interpretation of Husserl's Phenomenological Reduction," *Philosophy Today*, v. 27, Winter 1983, p. 342.

Yount, Mark, "Two Reversibilities: Merleau-Ponty and Derrida," *Philosophy Today*, v. 34, Summer 1990, p. 129.